THE PROFIT

A Concise Guide to Corporate and
Management Strategy Formulation,
Implementation & Sales Execution

Justin L. Lurie

FIVE LIONS PUBLISHING

HOUSTON, TEXAS - WELLINGTON, NEW ZEALAND

Publisher's Note:

This publication is designed to provide authoritative information in regard to subject matter covered. It is sold with the understanding that the publisher is not engaged in rendering legal, accounting, or other professional services. If you require legal advice or other expert assistance, you should seek the services of a competent professional.

UNITED STATES LIBRARY OF CONGRESS CATALOGING-IN-PUBLICATION DATA

NATIONAL LIBRARY OF NEW ZEALAND

Lurie, Justin L

   The Profit: A Concise Guide to Corporate and Management Strategy Formulation, Implementation & Sales Execution / Justin Lurie

   p. 195 cm.
   Includes bibliographical references and index.
   ISBN 978-0-473-29698-8

   1. Business Planning 2. Sales Executives 3. Corporate Profits

*EVERYTHING SHOULD BE MADE AS SIMPLE
AS POSSIBLE, BUT NOT SIMPLER*

ALBERT EINSTEIN

*SIMPLICITY IS THE ULTIMATE
SOPHISTICATION*

LEONARDO DA VINCI

Table of Contents

Preface 9

Section One: Strategy Best Practices 13

Who the company is, the vision, values, and goal setting 13

   Core Ideology 14

   Strategic Principle 17

   Goal Setting 20

   Mission Statements 24

Company Structure & Strategy 27

   Strategy Questions Framework 27

   Competitive Forces at Work 31

      Suppliers Creating Leverage 33

      Buyers Creating Leverage 35

      Will Our Products Be Replaced? 37

Measuring Strategy Performance 40

   How Did the Previous Years' Projections Compare with Reality? 40

   How to Fix the Projection vs Reality Gap 42

   Avoiding Common Strategy & Implementation Mistakes 47

Section Summary & Conclusion 51

Section Two: Does Your Current Business Model Need Refinement? 53

Defining the Business Model 54

When the Business Model Craves Change 60

Business Model Change Framework 62

Section Summary & Conclusion 62

Section Three: Aligning the Value Curve   **65**

Defining the Value Curve 66

   Benchmarking: The Good, The Bad, & The Ugly 69

The Value Curve in Practice 70

   Step One: Where Are We Now? 70

   Step Two: How to Find the Right Side of the Graph 71

      Field Work 72

      Creating New Curves 73

      Evaluating The New Ideas 76

      Taking Action 79

Who Isn't Purchasing From You & How to Attract Them 82

Section Summary & Conclusion 87

Section Four: Implementation &Buy-in   **89**

Not Just Hearing, But Believing: Achieving Buy-in 89

   Strategic Scorecard & Incentives 92

      Motivating Towards Execution 94

   Accountability & Expectations 96

   Internal Politics 97

      Common Hurdles 99

Teamwork for Maximum Effectiveness 100

   Multi-Disciplinary Teams 103

Fixing the Decision Making Bottleneck 104

   Principles to Making Good Decisions Quickly & Effectively ... 107

Framework to Evaluate Decision Making History 109

Section Summary & Conclusion 111

Section Five: Marketing Strategy **113**

Barriers to Market Adoption 114

    The Five A's 114

Think & Sell in a Narrative 114

    An Emotional Journey 116

    Creating the Narrative 119

Framing the Conversation 121

    All Publicity is Good Publicity? 122

    Descriptives & Taglines 124

Generating Word of Mouth Buzz 127

    Staying Top of Mind 128

    Monkey See, Monkey Do 131

Section Summary & Conclusion 133

Section Six: Sales Strategy Execution **137**

New Organizational Strategy, New Processes 138

    Evaluation Phase 139

    Designing the Improvement Process 142

        Building Best Practices 142

    Implementing the Sales Strategy 144

    Tracking & Measuring Results 146

Obtaining Leverage 147

Sales Leadership 150

Section Summary & Conclusion 152

Section Seven: Expanding Internationally 155

    Step-by-Step Expansion Plan 157

        Market Research Options 157

        Strategic Positioning Approaches for the Foreign Market 159

        Joint Ventures 163

    Complications to Know & Avoid 166

        Micro Factors to Control at Business Level 166

        Macro Factors, Adapting at Country Level 168

            Political Risk 169

            Economic & Social Risk 171

        Common Issues 173

    Global Decision Making 175

    Section Summary & Conclusion 177

Conclusion 181

Table of Figures 183

Bibliography 185

Index 191

Preface

What is Strategy? Why does it matter? How do I increase sales? Why don't we sell more?

These questions are asked at all levels of organizations, from entry level sales staff to senior management. Having a unified strategy that is clear, concise, and, most of all, understood by all members of the team - from the fresh-out-of-school to the CEO - is crucial for the strategy to actually be executed – not just discussed.

This book is a **clear and concise guide** on building your company's strategy, executing that strategy, and positioning your sales team for maximum effectiveness. Following this step-by-step guide will assist you in leading your company to greater profitability.

Like this preface, the writing style is short and to the point without technical jargon and academic prose. At the end of each chapter is a summary and 'action points' for greater practicability and efficiency for you, the reader, to translate concepts into action and then into profit.

In the following chapters you will find the step-by-step process to formulate the strategy, plan the execution, and then to train the sales staff accordingly.

We'll follow the fictional story of Roger Harrison, a senior executive at the oil and gas service company Ramicant Corporation, which is witnessing at best plateaued growth numbers. Roger wants, and needs, to make changes, but only has the political capital to take one big shot. Second chances are not given that often at Ramicant, so Roger wants an end-to-end strategy – a complete vision that is effective, will last more than one fiscal quarter, and is clear enough so that the entire company can believe and follow.

- - -

The Financial Collapse of 2007 to 2009 was both a disaster and a blessing for myself. The company where I was employed closed their retail commodity sales division as did the majority of the industry in New York; it was time to re-evaluate and find a new direction.

Selling physical and paper commodities such as natural gas, electricity, and petroleum products allows (or more accurately: forces) you to be creative in order to differentiate your company and product from the rest. One might think it is easy, just focus on price, service, and most of all, "the client gets me!" That doesn't work. You become as commoditized as the commodity you are selling.

This is where (and why) corporate strategy, execution and implementation, and instituting best practices to drive sales is most necessary. Almost every company puts great effort into making sure their product isn't viewed as a commodity, now try doing that with an actual commodity. The age old question, "How do you de-commodify a commodity?" This book will show you how to do just that.

My new professional calling came to me post TARP bailouts, Lehman Collapse, and the housing 'bubble.' It was to fine tune my strategic skills and share with as many companies as possible. Since then, I've consulted to create and refine the corporate strategy for organizations ranging from established multi-billion dollar companies to pre-sale startups who see the sky as the limit. Hence, the birth of a consultant, just the way every undergraduate dreams of their path – financial collapse to consultancy.

Section One: Strategy Best Practices

*Define what your brand stands for, its core values
and tone of voice, and then communicate
consistently in those terms.*

SIMON MAINWARING

Who the company is, the vision, values, and goal setting

If you were to describe your company today, would you define the products, rave about the MBAs and PhDs, or speak of the internal culture as would a cutting edge tech company? If we fast forward one hundred years and ask the same question to a person at your company in a similar role as yourself, how might they answer? If they chose any of the same paths of product description, the talent/people, or the atmosphere, would their answer be similar to yours?

Most likely, no. Company's products may change drastically from decade to decade, let alone in one hundred years. In the 19th Century, current mobile phone maker Nokia was a rubber producer, electricity generator, and ground wood pulp mill among other things. It took a long succession of industries and products to reach a

62.5% global market share for its mobile phone Symbian Operating System[1].

Without a doubt the people inside the company change often too, with greater frequency today than occurred in generations past. The concept of a 'company for life' is almost foreign for many in the private sector, especially for those below the age of forty. In the future, why assume the leadership wants or needs to hire only those with advanced degrees? Or those who can speak three languages, or are able to lift heavy objects? Could they do more with less? With technology, the needs and wants of companies change, sometimes drastically.

Culture: think Mad Men. If Don Draper were to describe his sexist whiskey swirling office culture of 1960s Madison Avenue in Manhattan, would it describe where you work today? If you're in a Western culture, most likely no. The norms and culture change with the times and with generations. For example, former head of the National Security Agency (NSA) General Michael Hayden recruited 'hackers' to use their special skills for the United States Government by visiting 'techie' trade shows and conferences. General Hayden, a 41 year military veteran, wanted to match the culture and look less 'government' or traditional, so he wore jeans and a t-shirt. Reuters[2] news service described the newly recruited personnel as having "purple hair, tie-dyed shirts, and blue jeans." Could this change of culture at the NSA have been foreseen twenty years earlier?

Core Ideology

To best position your company, it is important to understand

1   http://en.wikipedia.org/wiki/Nokia
2   http://www.reuters.com/article/2013/06/07/us-usa-cyberwar-idUS-BRE95608D20130607

who you are at the core. What aspects of your company are, and should not, be changing? The Core Ideology is your raison d'etre, your reason for being and for doing. It is what you stand for, who you are.

This ideal or core should be consistent across generations, and does not sway with the fads of time or industry. The Core Ideology is bigger than any personality or leadership at control of the firm, and also beyond the greatest product or service that your company offers this day or the next. Remember Nokia's evolution, what if the company had decided its raison d'etre was to be a rubber maker one hundred years ago?

The Core Ideology is the essential purpose, the reason for existing as an organization. It will provide long-term guidance to the strategic direction of the company to assist in moving forward. It is not a business strategy, nor a specific goal, but instead an ideal.

The Water Project[3] facilitates construction of water wells and water projects throughout Africa. The Water Project is not a construction company, it is not a water company, and it is not forever limited to Africa. Instead, it has a Core Ideology of helping people live better lives by facilitating something necessary for survival. This ideology should last generations, and it can certainly expand to other regions or other products, such as facilitating or providing medicine, food, and/or shelter in Haiti. Their Core Ideology is to improve life at the basic necessity level.

The United States Constitution is another example of a Core Ideology as a symbol of shared values and direction for a very large organization – a country. This document has endured for over two hundred years, and hopefully will for at least another two hundred. It has provided a reference point to judge new legislation, and for assessment of rights, responsibilities, and checks on power as the original framers intended. How could this compare to your own company? Is there a Core Ideology to keep the

---

3   http://thewaterproject.org/or-water-projects

company on track no matter the current product or leadership/ President?

An office supply company's Core Ideology is not "to sell pencils and pens," but instead "to provide the tools for business to be conducted."

A cargo shipping company does not have a Core Ideology of "moving giant container loads or boxes from port to port," but instead to facilitate safe and reliable international commerce."

Viewing the Core Ideology in a different light within the Oil & Gas industry, Southwestern Energy is known for their core value statement of "The Right People Doing the Right Things" in combination with "Wisely investing the cash flow from the underlying assets" will create "outstanding value." This statement will outlive the product fads, leadership styles or personalities. Instead of focusing on the product directly, it is a focus on teamwork and dedication to produce exceptional results.

Let us now introduce our fictional friend, Roger Harrison, a senior executive of Ramicant Corporation, an Oil & Gas services company based in Houston, Texas. Roger is tasked with rejuvenating the stagnating company as soon as possible. Knowing that he likely has only one opportunity to succeed due to the political environment of his peers, his goal is to plan out the entire strategy and execute at 100% implementation.

Roger's first step is to define Ramicant's Core Ideology. Now that he has a firm grasp of the concept and why it is important (to know where you're going in the future), he will begin the exercise. For best results, since many minds are better than one, Roger asked a group of his peers and a few managers to join him in the conference room.

Roger asked the room the following question:

We make XYZ products, and provide ABC services, but why is this important?

And why is that first answer important?

He had each person individually write down three to five ideas or suggestions within five minutes. He then wrote the answers/concepts on a white board for all to see. After discussing and identifying what they believe might be their core ideologies, they asked these questions:

1. If you were to start a new company today, would you want to take these concepts with you?

2. If these core ideologies were of a person, not a company or organization, would you want to be associated with this person?

3. If you lived another 100 years, would these ideologies be relevant, or would you want them to be?

4. If it were a competitive disadvantage, would you still want to hold these core ideologies?

Strategic Principle

"Make it Simple, But Significant"

-Don Draper, Mad Men

The next step is to define the Strategic Principle; it is action oriented and provides clear and unambiguous guidance for many decisions. Simultaneously, it allows employees the freedom to make decisions, although within a clear set of confines. Here are a few corporate examples:

WAL-MART: "LOW PRICES, EVERY DAY"

GENERAL ELECTRIC: "BE #1 OR #2 IN EVERY INDUSTRY WE COMPETE IN, OR GET OUT"

SOUTHWEST AIRLINES: "MEET CUSTOMERS SHORT-HAUL TRAVEL NEEDS AT FARES COMPETITIVE WITH THE COST OF AUTOMOBILE TRAVEL"

These very pithy, direct, and yet descriptive Strategic Principles provide an unmistakable direction for the company. The Strategic Principle answers whether a new action, direction, project, or endeavor will fit in the direction of the company. This is also a test of the strategic strength of an action or decision.

The key is being memorable, so everyone knows it and lives it daily. When Southwest Airlines is considering creating a new route between cities, they take into consideration their clear objective and determine if this new project is a fit. If we add an extra set of peanuts per passenger, will the cost be more expensive than packing up the kids into the station wagon or SUV?

This eliminates many stages of management decision making, which translates into saved time, saved internal costs, increased nimbleness, and empowered employees. For multinational organizations, managers cannot always wait for decisions to be made by headquarters in a distant country due to internal process and review, time zones, event calendars, etc.

The Strategic Principle is also a management training tool to keep the entire organization advancing in the same direction. If new managers are not fully trained or acclimated to their new role, they always have a rule and direction to fall back on to overcome their lack of experience or information.

One of the great commonalities across all industries is consistent technological change, when this happens is your management team prepared? Change can occur overnight when a new website replaces your product or function as a free service or free software app, among many other operational changes or possibilities. The same question exists for internal leadership change - regardless of the turmoil, holding true to the Strategic Principle should provide guidance to make sound business decisions.

After Roger and his team discovered and defined their core ideologies, he is now ready to create Ramicant's Strategic Principle – their strategy and action guiding statement. First step, ask the group:

A. How does Ramicant differentiate itself from the competition?

B. What is the substitution from your product or industry?

For example, instead of flying, one could drive, ride the train, etc.

C. What does the firm want to accomplish?

Using the answers from above, is there a clear principle that emerges that can tie one, two, or three of the thoughts together? If so, test the principle with these questions:

Is it pithy, memorable, and obvious?

Does this portray a five year vision, or a forever horizon?

Is it actionable, does it tell you or the staff what should be done or achieved?

Does it guide the organization to the same point or direction?

Can this be used as a framework against which decisions are made?

A key to implementing the Strategic Principle is keeping it very short and simple in order to be memorable and understandable, which will then translate into actionable. When the principle is too long or overly wordsmithed, it becomes hard to digest and internalize. It can become 'just another' corporate mantra that is borne to be forgotten. No one lives and breathes statements they don't listen to, comprehend, remember or believe affects them.

Internal repetition from top executives to managers to front line employees will also be key. Wal-Mart keeps their message front and center via broadcasting it on advertisements, store signage, and even on their t-shirts. Consistency, simplicity, and repetition.

The Strategic Principle may not last 50 years or 100 years as a Core Ideology could, but instead could be reviewed annually or bi-annually. As the market and the company evolves due to technology, changes of culture and taste, or regulatory change, so can the decision making framework and the direction of the company.

Goal Setting

"If you want to build a ship, don't drum up the men to gather wood, divide the work and give orders. Instead, teach them to yearn for the vast and endless sea."

Antoine de Saint – Exupery, (1900-1944), Author, Aviator, Poet

A few weeks before the college football season begins a coach gathers his players around the locker room and asks everyone to state their goal for the upcoming season. The first player said, "I want to finish above .500 and win more games than we lose." His teammate next to him rose to speak and said, "I plan on heading to a Bowl Game!" The next player with even more enthusiasm said, "I want to win the Bowl Game!" At the end of room, after all of the other teammates have spoken the final player stood up and said "I don't understand how any of you could even conceive of just finishing near .500, or just attending a Bowl Game. I'm here to win the National Championship and anything short of that is a disappointment."

What you believe to be, or should be, the obvious and clear goal is not always shared among your team or company as a whole. Everyone has their own internal biases and motivations, and certainly carries the baggage of previous experiences. The first player who stated he wanted to finish above .500 and have more wins than losses may be the most experienced player on the team and remembers the previous season's record of only one win and nine losses. The final player who inspirationally spoke of winning the National Championship or bust, may only be a freshman and has yet to play a collegiate match. Perspective, experience, motivation, and biases will determine your staff, or team's, goals unless management makes these proper goals and visions abundantly clear. This section will show you how.

For many years strategy was stamped as a management function, just another task to do throughout the day such as answering letters or making sure the employees clocked in. Recognizing that strategy is essential to an organization's success, or the lack thereof might result in failure, strategy evolved to become a unique discipline.

At its most basic level, strategy is a choice – a specific choice to position to win. Strategy is not a vision of where the organization wants or believes it should be, that is the goal. Strategy is also not reforming and recasting in the same direction to gain greater efficiencies in the name of value, this is optimizing and not winning. Strategy is making choices to achieve the goal.

An effective goal is contradictory in scope but never in results. The goal is short and obvious, but at the same time must be all encompassing and detailed. Every region, discipline, and employee must have their own goal, including, and in addition to, the organizational goal. The individual goals must be actionable: every steak must be cooked to the exact degree, every bus must run on time, all software is bug free, all drill bits are assembled and delivered with precision.

The overall goal must be to win – although it is up to management to define what a 'win' entails - whether that is market share, year-on-year revenue growth, entering a foreign market, or something entirely different. Take great caution if any of the above listed definitions are the goal, for it misses the crucial nature of what a goal must represent.

The goal must be a vision that all can share, see, and strive towards daily in every aspect of their roles and duties. There needs to be a picture that all can relate to. If your company's leader addressed the entire organization at a conference behind the podium and said "we need 10% revenue growth every quarter!" who would applaud? Who would rise to their feet? What if the goal was 20% a quarter? More would ignore rather than be inspired.

Instead of a revenue growth goal, what if your company's leader said "We are going to land on an asteroid and bring the raw materials back to Earth and we'll be the richest company ever created!" Would you applaud? Did your heart beat faster? Would Tom from accounting, or Bill from R&D be excited to show up to work the next day?

Did you create a mental image of landing on the asteroid? (Depending on the year you read this book will determine how daring this goal is.) The goal must be a very pithy and vivid description that translates into a vision that all can see. Henry Ford's vision was for roads filled with cars, not horses. NetJets has a vision of fleets of private jets crisscrossing the sky providing private airline travel for the many, not the few. Create an emotional connection between the product the company provides and the big picture of what everyone can achieve and win together. Include passion, create an environment where employees want to be a part of the goal and to fulfill their duties with fervor.

Think beyond the current resources or the current market size, imagine the goal with at least a ten year horizon. Think Big. To be a visionary doesn't always mean you are practical for the current day, but step outside of the confines of the current thinking or the current technology. Step your mind back into the relatively recent year 1990, could you imagine explaining two of the most popular and valuable companies in today's world to a friend or colleague: Facebook and Google?

It is easy to be caught up in the visionary aspects of a goal, but it is also extremely tactical and strategic. There cannot be a guarantee of success, for if it was simple it is then unworthy of being vision-ary; the staff, ranging from the executives to the entry level, must all believe the goal can be accomplished. To accomplish the goals, each level of the organization must be assigned achievable goals that will build into the multi-year vision on the horizon.

These goals are to be actionable, similar to those listed above such as cooking a steak to the right temperature for every order, but the following level goal is to reach the next hill, and then to climb the next mountain. The organization has a path and a vi-sion to aim for the stars over the next decade, but needs to climb this hill, and then that mountain next. Actionable, achievable, and visionary.

When companies are young and trending upwards quickly there is often great enthusiasm and vigor. Sometimes the goal is an IPO and many people becoming wealthy past the 4pm market close. Other goals are an acquisition by a larger company. What hap-pens after that first major goal or vision is met?

More mature companies can become complacent and have a lack of significant new innovations, which can lead to a lack of fervor or push. How to replace this new culture and inspire the organi-zation?

When the drive has vanished companies need a new encompassing goal and vision. "Now that we have landed on the asteroid, it is time we land on Mars!" Encore performance, push the edge of the envelope further. When should this speech be given about the encore to Mars? After winning the Super Bowl, how long until coaches go back to work?

After landing on the asteroid and bringing the minerals back to Earth to achieve fabulous wealth, it is time to gather all employees together again. The timing is a judgment call for there should be time to celebrate the achievement(s). However, the next goal needs to be set so the team can be refocused and re-determined.

Mission Statements

The Mission Statement is often misunderstood and can be an improperly used tool. It is often long, robust in verboseness, rarely understood, and seldom memorized or even read. Since the Mission Statement is a tool, it should be treated as one – another device to achieve your goal via effective strategy.

Here is an example of what not to do:

> *Our mission is to operate the best specialty retail business in America, regardless of the product we sell. Because the product we sell is books, our aspirations must be consistent with the promise and the ideals of the volumes which line our shelves. To say that our mission exists independent of the product we sell is to demean the importance and the distinction of being booksellers. As booksellers we are determined to be the very best in our business, regardless of the size, pedigree or inclinations of our competitors. We will continue to bring our industry nuances of style and approaches to bookselling*

which are consistent with our evolving aspirations.
Above all, we expect to be a credit to the communi-
ties we serve, a valuable resource to our customers,
and a place where our dedicated booksellers can
grow and prosper. Toward this end we will not only
listen to our customers and booksellers but embrace
the idea that the Company is at their service.

This is the Mission Statement from Barnes & Nobles, Inc. Not only is it long, unhelpful, and probably foreign to their staff, it is also contradictory. Not a crime for being boring, but worthless as a tool. The Core Ideology describes the organizations' essence as to who they are so they know where to head in the future, the Strategic Principle gives actionable guidance to make decisions, and the Mission Statement describes your current tasks and offerings.

Below is Amazon's Mission Statement:

To be the Earth's most customer-centric company,
where customers can find and discover anything
they might want to buy online

This describes the day-to-day ambitions of a company and their operations. It is not about the greater purpose of the company in comparison to a pharmaceutical company's Core Ideology of 'Helping Society Live Healthy Lives.' The Mission Statement is the product or service offered, but not what the product or service means.

The Mission Statement is still aspirational and not readily achievable when presented correctly. The New York Public Library's Mission Statement describes their daily goals and offerings succinctly, but could use more definitive descriptors, such as who the communities are:

To inspire lifelong learning, advance knowledge, and
strengthen our communities.

Roger decided he wants to abandon Ramicant's current long worded Mission Statement and create a new document from scratch. The new Mission Statement will be easy to read, understand, and internalize so the staff can have a reminder of the daily activities, not just the long-term vision.

To build the Mission Statement, answer the four questions below and build into a concise model. Roger inserted his answers:

Q. What do we do?

A. *Provide Oil Field Services*

Q. How do we do it?

A. *Exceptional Customer Service*

Q. Whom do we do it for?

A. *Exploration & Production Companies, Operators, Drillers*

Q. What value are we bringing today?

A. *Cost Effective Supplies to Save Money*

If you believe these answers are dreadful, it is because they are. Roger realizes it too once he had an honest look back at his answers. What does 'exceptional customer service' mean? Perhaps to Ramicant employee John who answered his 150th phone call of the day it means something different than to Roger who answers five phone calls a month from a customer. Ramicant has goals, so use this Mission Statement to help direct the short term and daily goals into a useful tool.

What do we do?

Ramicant creates pumps, compressors, blowers, and fans

How do we do it?

Significant R&D, 3-day order turnaround time, mass market and customized solutions

Whom do we do it for?

Oil and Gas companies who operate in domestic US, concentrating on Texas, Oklahoma, Colorado, and Gulf of Mexico. Small independents to Super Majors purchase from Ramicant

What value are we bringing today?

Cost per quality. It is high quality machines competing at the same price as low quality competitors. Turnaround time is fast, mechanical guarantees are superior.

In combination, Roger wanted it short yet helpful. His final draft of a Mission Statement is:

"Quickly delivering exceptionally designed & serviced fluid transfer machines anywhere oil and gas needs to be extracted and processed in the USA"

Roger's team will remember to assemble products correctly the first time so they won't have to service poorly constructed equipment in the field if there is breakage. All parts must be delivered quickly, and Ramicant will sell across the USA, aspiring beyond the regional borders of today.

Company Structure & Strategy

Strategy Questions Framework

Strategy is more than just developing aspirational quotes, visions, or an all-encompassing goal. Strategy includes developing frameworks, organizational structures, and,most of all, the execution. To develop frameworks and structures, the first steps are to answer two of the very basic questions:

1. What Business(es) Should We Be In?

2. How Do We Allocate Our Resources to Achieve the Goals for each Business?

The first question may sound obvious at the general level for an established company, but break it down two or three levels. For example, should Microsoft be in the Tablet business or Apple be a book retailer via iTunes? On a smaller level, should the local gardener also handle large tree trimming? Or, should a mega multinational Exploration and Production company like ExxonMobil also sell retail gasoline?

In allocating resources, the organization as a whole should not always look to each division or segment as individual non-integrated pieces of the company. The segments or various units in combination with the functions, such as distribution or accounting, from each business line can work together to reach the total goals via enhanced operational effectiveness and/or interdependency with customers.

Operational effectiveness is gained efficiencies and continual improvement in every value point that is benchmarked against the competition. Although this is important in some degrees, and unimportant in others (more on this topic in later chapters), this is not a complete strategy. If consistently benchmarking against the competition, the competitive convergence[4] from imitation becomes inevitable. Companies begin to resemble others in offerings, quality, and the value offered. Managers need to not compete on the benchmark versus benchmark and look at the larger picture of how to achieve their vision, and be profitable. Do not consider how to sell more "Happy Meals,"

---

4   (Porter, What is Strategy 1996)

but consider instead how to make more money.

Being lean has clear and definite advantages in profitability and the agile ability to move and flex with market changes, but this cannot be the goal. The concept is integrating the units and the divisions to a position where your competitors cannot copy a few of the lean methodologies or efficiencies as they could copy product features, nor could they copy or replicate the company wide-organization and positioning of internal and external interactions.

For example, Michael Porter in 'What is Strategy' outlines Ikea's system of strategic activities that positions Ikea uniquely and strongly against its competitors. Ikea focuses on four main points:

1. Self-selection by customers

2. Limited customer service

3. Modular furniture design

4. Low manufacturing cost

There are sixteen additional subtasks and actions to support Ikea's core framework, each activity fits and supports another. To name a few:

A. Year round stocking

B. In-house design focused on cost of manufacturing

C. Suburban locations with ample parking

D. Kit packaging

The organizational structure itself is the competitive advantage – it is designed to be unique and well positioned to compete and win business in their market and industry. The key is designing the system so it cannot easily be replicated by a competing firm. For example, if Ikea has a particular couch (or other product) that is extremely popular and selling tremendous amounts of inventory, competitors cannot just copy the design and/or material and be successful as they might be by mimicking features of a competitor's mobile phone on their own. A competing company would need to change its entire functional system to integrate into a cohesive unit like Ikea in order to compete and hope to win in a complete value proposition. Positioning based on structures and systems are far more secure than those based on individual products and/or actions. The retailers are competing not just product to product, but system to system too. Ikea offers not just a product, but a price value and shopping experience (points listed A through D) that cannot be easily replicated.

Using a different method from Ikea, Procter & Gamble used their people as the basis of their cross-integration and strategic positioning. Procter & Gamble combined their staff from marketing, manufacturing, logistics, finance, IT, and HR into a customer team to force integration with their largest customers, such as Target and Wal-Mart.

The goal was to understand the customer so well that they could work collaboratively to develop and execute mutual business goals, and to have mutual interdependence for years, ensuring a long-term customer and steady cash flow. This is an example of Joint Value Creation and a shared action plan to win.

Using the talent of Procter & Gamble and working closely to find the needs of their customers, they found efficiencies and cost savings in the supply chain and developed action plans to drive more customers into stores to purchase more product. A win – win, or joint value.

A new deodorant can be copied or replicated, a new toothpaste with features of teeth whitening is often copied, but attempting company-to-company integration with the largest product retailers would be extremely difficult. The strategy is integration and operational effectiveness for joint profit.

Competitive Forces at Work

There will always be competition in varying degrees and levels. Albeit, when a new product is invented or a new industry is conceived, there may be little initial competition. Inevitably, there will always be competition for a successful product in the long run either directly or indirectly via substitutes.

If there is no competition, it may be time to evaluate how worthwhile your endeavor truly is. Where there is value and profit, there will be competition from new entrants attempting to create their own revenue pie or firms wanting to create your product or service internally.

Consistently learn more about your competition by reading newspapers, journals, etc., try their products, and talk to their customers. Maintain a presence at trade shows and/or industry events and engage socially with the competitors at the minimum when in the same room.

Consider these positioning questions to evaluate your current direct competition:

A. What can both of our organizations do/perform?

B. What our organization can do, but the competitor cannot?

C. What the competitor can do, but our organization cannot?

This information may seem obvious at the moment, but it will be invaluable in later chapters as you discover and expand your value curves. For now, contemplate the basics of your competitive situation as we discuss the four major forces that shape and beget industry competition.

Michael Porter's article 'Five Competitive Forces That Shape Strategy' outlines these building blocks, in their adapted form, as listed below:

A. Threat of New Entrants

B. Bargaining Power of Suppliers

C. Bargaining Power of Buyers

D. Threat of Substitute Products or Services

If profits are high or very healthy, there will be intense competition to steal market share away from the leader. To counteract this new or potential competition, the existing market leader must create a deterrent or series of deterrents so competing firms view too much risk and not enough reward. An example of a strong deterrent is the The L Brand's (formerly known as the Limited Brands) retail outlet Victoria's Secret, the middle market King (or Queen) of ladies lingerie. Victoria's Secret's outstanding branding has an emphasis on selling a combination of luxury, fashion, the latest technological and scientific advances in lingerie (think support), and creating celebrities out of their models. A difficult hill to climb for any mid-market competitor.

Gisele Bundchen and Alessandra Ambrosio have become household names and forever linked to Victoria's Secret as 'Angels,' and are shown along with other Angels during their annual internationally televised fashion show. Their lingerie products go well beyond the traditional marketing and advertising concepts of 'Features, Advantages, and Benefits,' that can easily be replicated and copied by actual and potential competitors. Instead, Victoria's Secret has built a substantial brand that has entered into pop culture through creating a replaceable pool of celebrities, by naming new Angels and by churning previous models through and out.

To compete in the mid-market lingerie industry, a competitor would need to unseat one of the most recognizable brands in America, and overcome pop-culture celebrities to do so. A challenging task and a tremendous deterrent.

When the suppliers hold many of the chips, to no surprise they also hold the power. When there are very few suppliers of the finished goods but many retailers to sell the product, there is a strong possibility of a high margin supplier and low margin retailer.

Apple's iPhone is an exceptionally popular tool, toy, and communication device rolled into one. There is a vast array of electronic or specialty retailers such as Best Buy, telecommunication companies (the phone network themselves), kiosks in malls, or hundreds of websites to purchase the iPhone, but there is a limited number of phone networks to use the iPhone. There is great competition to purchase the iPhone as a consumer, and a reasonable level of competition between the phone carriers such as Verizon, Sprint, or AT&T, but yet there is still only one iPhone maker – Apple. The retailers fight and claw for very small margins whereas Apple's technology and brand drives the demand and enjoys the real markup and power over the market, capturing the true value.

Suppliers Creating Leverage

If your company is a supplier and has a need to position itself for greater leverage and profitability, consider situations where your product or service does not need to have the same exceptional brand name and/or consumer demand of an Apple product, but can still command a premium:

First, when there is a high cost to switch from one supplier to another. This does not always mean a higher cost of goods or great risk of damaging meaningful relationships, but instead the learning curve to use the new tools or product would be great. For example, a Bloomberg Terminal is a very powerful financial services information portal that requires a steep learning curve to adapt to the less than intuitive processes and intricacies. Switching to a new platform or software program such as Thomson Reuters would require learning a new set of processes, and code words to navigate, and finding where the necessary time sensitive information is located. Not an easy switch.

Within the Oil & Gas industry there are many subcontractors working on large projects who share the production facilities with the lead or head contractor. For the lead contractor to remove the subcontractor will require transferring all of the equipment, tools, and perhaps inventory out of the shared space and causing disruption for the larger company, especially if they need the tools owned by the company being replaced. The key for the smaller company: integration builds interdependence and value.

The second concept of positioning yourself for greater leverage is to create a specialized or intellectual property protected product. When a pharmaceutical drug company has a unique and patent protected pill it is difficult for the hospital or health care system to replace it with less expensive substitutes that will not perform to the same standards or expectations. Though this may sound obvious in healthcare, it can also be applied to high tech companies who build microchips using nanotechnology, or, on an industrial scale, a unique instrument to measure underground pipeline leaks. All valuable products that have leverage when setting prices and fees.

The third method of having leverage as a supplier is to have no substitutes at all. The United States federal government does not have a replacement – at least not today or tomorrow. The government has power if they are the supplier of land, access, leases, titles, or any other government selling to business transaction. Obviously you can't make your company more like the government, nor should you want to, but keep the theory in mind. Labor unions also have a similar clout for their members presumably have no replacements in highly specialized types of fields such as Railroad Engineers, or City School Teachers – it would be extremely difficult to replace an entire school district of teachers or send children to surrounding towns/cities.

The fourth method of suppliers' creating leverage is through the threat of entering the market themselves and cutting out the retailer or the middlemen. For a generation, Sony has been known as a premium home entertainment (stereos, TV, and even the Walkman) manufacturer and sold only through retail stores such as Best Buy or Circuit City. Sony has a reasonable argument that they can use their already existing direct to consumer marketing that drives consumers to their retail store partners for purchase, and/or redirect those consumers to Sony's website for purchase securing higher margins for themselves, or they can build retail stores in select cities where existing sales are already strong and again secure larger margins. This threat of entry and cutting out the retailer will provide Sony with leverage over their retail store partners.

Buyers Creating Leverage

The buyers have power beyond just choosing between vendors who address their scope or need best, or who may advertise the lowest or best price. The purchasers can also force higher quality and greater service of the contending suppliers in a competitive situation. In the following situations the buyers will have superior leverage over the supplier:

When there are few purchasing opportunities, or a limited number of buyers who purchase the products, the leverage will be gained by the buyer. The suppliers only have a few chances to win business and likely cannot afford to let opportunities slip by. This is common in industries with high fixed costs such as Offshore and Deepwater Drilling, or internet backbone hardware. When the competition is intense to sell products with a high fixed cost it results often in a low margin for the seller.

In a second example of buyers holding leverage, when the products for sale have reached near commodity status with little or no differentiation this will result in little power for the supplier. In an extreme example, a basic handheld calculator was a powerful and expensive tool a few decades ago. Firms would advertise, differentiate, and win the business for high cost and high margin calculators. Today, it is hard to imagine an advertisement for a handheld calculator or similar device. Thousands are still sold today albeit many are promotional items with company's logos or messages applied to the cover. The brand printing on the calculator may or may not be a commodity, but the device certainly is with high substitution. When the product is easily replaceable, or has few switching costs in switching between vendors – regardless of the commodity status or characteristic – the buyer will have strong leverage over the purchaser.

FIGURE 1: HEWLETT-PACKARD 35, FROM 1972

The final circumstance to be addressed here of how the buyer creates and maintains leverage is the threat of creating or making the purchased product in-house. Restaurants do not always need to purchase their desserts from the same suppliers from whom they purchase the steaks, frozen chicken, vegetables, or other ingredients they use to prepare the entrees and appetizers. Many diners in New York create exceptional cakes, cookies, cheesecakes and puddings in their kitchens although they purchase a tremendous range of products from the supplier/distributor to fulfill the extensive menu and product offerings, 24 hours a day, 7 days a week.

This method is by no means limited to just restaurants or small business, it can be applied to major corporations too. In a cost cutting move, Delta Airlines improved the technical capabilities within their own hangars by creating parts and tools to service their fleet instead of purchasing replacement pieces from the manufacturer, Boeing. Over time, Boeing recognized this threat from the industry as a whole and developed new supplier replacement programs to curb the loss of this post-sale fleet service market.

Will Our Products be Replaced?

In 1775 when the precursor to the United States Postal Service was formed, it was inconceivable that the major threat to the organization (beyond pension obligations) would be electronic communications –email, text message, FTP uploads/downloads, and cloud storage. Instead of mailing or shipping a box full of documents, they can be scanned, uploaded, stored on a server, and accessed anywhere in the world.

Companies such as FedEx or UPS didn't replace the Postal Service; those companies do not make door-to-door deliveries in the same sense or consistently carry the same type of goods. Could you imagine the shipper's cost for UPS to deliver junk mail door by door per zip code?

Substitutes are practically replacing the Postal Service. They are not just different products, but different methods. Skype and video conferencing has replaced some business travel and made time more efficient by eliminating drive, fly, airport and hotel expenses, and time. Travel agents have largely been replaced by websites such as Expedia, Orbitz, or Kayak. Booking is no longer even a phone call away, but instead just a few clicks from your mobile phone or computer.

Other traditional industries are being set back too, Netflix has replaced many consumers' need of Cable or Satellite TV (DirecTV, Dish) programming and costly monthly subscriptions. Seeing this trend, among others, has prompted cable company consolidations, including merging the United States two largest operators Time Warner and Comcast. Additionally, DirecTV and AT&T have also proposed merging.

The threat of a substitute is high when there is a reasonable method or product to fulfill the same purpose with a lower cost, superior contractual terms, or exceptional ease of use. Travel agents have been substituted by website programs due to at least one of these factors, arguably two – depending on your travel agent. It is very simple to book a flight and hotel at your convenience and view pictures online, compare prices, reviews, and select flight times. Having an agent read each review, describe hotel photos, and explain the myriad of flight time choices could be an arduous task. No hold times, or office hours on internet bookings either.

Roger is considering these many principles and factors of both the buy -side and sell-side of the equation and how he can position Ramicant strategically so he can minimize his negative exposure and expand his profit potential. With the thought of Ramicant as a supplier to Oil & Gas companies operating throughout the United States, he began with the most basic bullet points for himself to remember:

    A. Ramicant is a supplier: maintain leverage

B. Understand how the buyers will want to deleverage Ramicant and think ahead to prevent this from happening.

Next, build the framework to evaluate current and potential vulnerabilities, and also to begin to find competitive advantages (leverage):

    A. Can our product be easily replaced via competition or substitute?

    B. Is our product highly specialized where a competitor cannot replicate it?

    C. What pains would our [current or potential] customer have to switch from us, or switch to us?

    D. Could our clients' create our product or service in-house?

    E. Is our product now, or will soon, become a commodity in the market?

    F. How many potential purchasers are there within our target market, is this a small or large potential?

    G. Can we market or set our sights past the middleman and sell directly to the end user?

Measuring Strategy Performance

How Did the Previous Years' Projections Compare with Reality?

When was the last time your company reviewed and compared the strategy from one, two, or three years ago against the actual performance? Michael Mankins & Richard Steele's[5] research on this subject noted only 15% of companies make it a regular practice to go back and compare the expectations versus the results for each unit in the prior years' strategic plan.

The most effective method to make accurate future predictions and a winning strategic direction is to know your true capabilities and how well they will actually correlate to your assumptions. Making pie in the sky assumptions and sales predictions are easy, making them actually happen is an entirely different challenge. What was your company's management 'batting average' in predicting performance, or do you not know?

In theory, how could you be confident of your strategic direction if you cannot trust the accuracy of the performance assumptions?

When the firm is unaware of the accuracy of the projections, there is a possibility the strategic direction is headed down the wrong lane, essentially throwing good money after bad. If the strategy and/or subsequent execution is poor, it may be time to find a new direction and options.

Should the medium or long-term results not make the expectations or projections, then senior management's sales and financial forecasts become inaccurate and out of sync. This could have significant effects for publicly traded companies if promised results are not met, or are strongly below expectations.

Mankins & Steele detail the lack of control over the firm's internal portfolio management due to either scarcity of reporting or absence of review versus projection. If business segments cannot be properly evaluated, how could a manager know whether to keep the units or sell the segment? If there is a negative value, holding onto the asset is a net negative and hurts the firm not only in net result, but also in opportunity cost by allocating funds and resources for a sinking ship instead of a potential rising star.

If the staff believes the plan, performance, or metric to evaluate the strategy is unrealistic, then not only credibility is lost, but also the plan. The overall goal and actions needed to reach it will be ignored and labeled as pie in the sky. Basically the strategy is dead in the water. Over time if this cycle is repeated and there are no consequences, then the next strategy, and the strategy after that will also be ignored and significant change or growth does not occur.

The projection needs to match reality to remain credible.

Should the expectations not be met it is common to see staff ranging from entry level to senior management duck for cover and pass the blame. Experienced staff will see the inevitability of fallout coming their way should there be a cycle of not reaching projections, and spend more of their time CYA[6] then being creative and motivated to execute senior management's strategy. To state the obvious, for a company to be successful "staff must spend more time executing strategy then finding ways to avoid getting fired."

Only 63% is the average realized performance[7] of a strategy, meaning there is an average of 37% performance loss within strategy execution. In other words, expect only about two-thirds

---

6   Cover Your Butt (not really those exact words)
7   Turning Great Strategy into Great Performance (Steele 2009)

of your strategy to be executed as planned. Why do you lose approximately 37% of the strategy execution? There are a variety of factors as researched by Steele & Mankins.The highlights are: 7.5% of the performance loss is due to inadequate or unavailable resources, 5.2% is due to poorly communicating the strategy, 4.5% is lack of clear actions to take, and 4.1% is not defining accountabilities for action.

When the performance is far off from the projection, is this the fault of the strategy and projection, or, is there an error in execution? How can senior management determine if the strategy is weak planning, mediocre execution, all of the above, or none? The best answer is obviously not to get into this situation.

An autopsy may need to be performed to find the weak link(s) and to answer the following series of questions. Have the recommended actions at the senior, middle, and worker level been carried out as planned or required? Were there any warning signs that should not have been ignored regarding performance?

Were the available or the assigned resources used correctly, or should the distribution of talent, management, funds, supplies/tools, have been rearranged?

How to Fix the Projection vs Reality Gap

Providing a practical and yet innovative strategy and projection is the theme of this book, it is a combination of the many chapters and proposed ideas. On the very specific area of accurate projections, here are a few rules and guidelines.

First, the strategy must be easily comprehended and presented. Eliminate confusion and state the clear end goal (see earlier in this Section describing vision and goals), and delineate the path to reach it with what is and is not included in the strategy (to be further elaborated in coming Sections).

It is vital to recognize in the planning process that there are competing inherent biases and financial rewards between departments/divisions and levels of the ladder. For example, Operations Departments may focus on issues that affect their statistical evaluations and that influence their financial bonus' and/or ability to move up the corporate ladder. Same with sales, finance, and most other divisions. The CEO often has a separate performance metric (price per share, 5 year growth average, etc.) than the other managers. If the corporate strategy needs final approval from the Board of Directors, the Board will also have their own biases as to whether it is a myopic metric focused on a discipline or legal obligation, stock price, or on a viable general ten-year horizon or projection.

The key is to be familiar with all of these competing interests and to understand their thoughts and actions. In the case when managers are issued bonuses for short term results, the planned projection for the immediate term may be under-served or under-valued so this expectation can be exceeded with minimal change (or effort) resulting in financial gain for the planners. In the same company, should the CEO or Board of Directors be compensated for long-term projections –without actually achieving the long-term results – the projection will unsurprisingly have a steep curve towards the sky. What is the result? Naturally an unrealistic projection in generating a hockey stick graph.

FIGURE 2: ANNUAL STRATEGY ATTEMPTS FAILURE

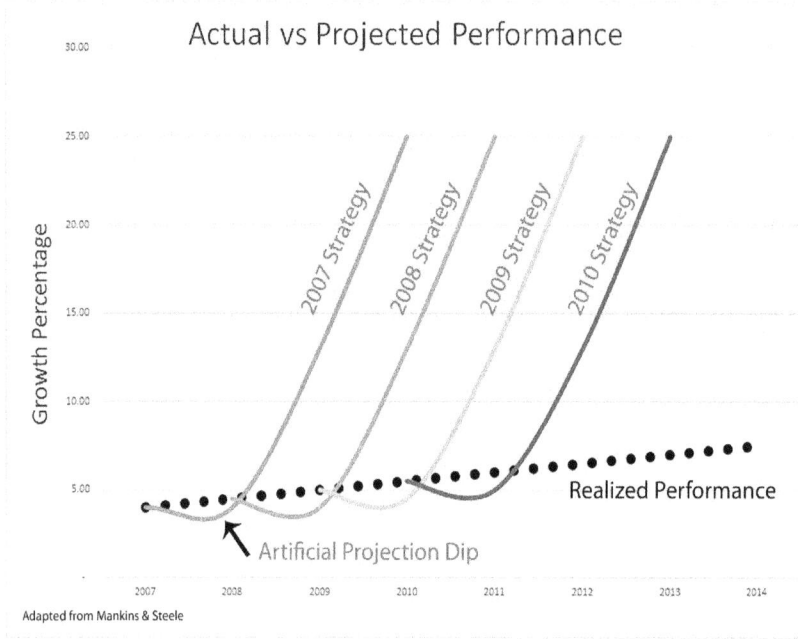

Actual vs Projected Performance

Adapted from Mankins & Steele

Market research cannot be excluded from the formation of projections for these conditions are equally important to the financial projections. Sales figures and revenue must be realistic and additional purchasers within a market cannot just be invented. For example, if there are only 3 million people in the geographic region where your store(s) are located, it is unrealistic to plan to sell to 4 million people, unless internet sales are included.

Prior to implementation of the strategy and forecast, decide when key resources will need to be active and/or ready. For example, if the strategy is to open a new market by extending into the State of California and sales professionals are needed on the ground to complete deals, then hiring additional sales people must be a priority. Through the upfront planning process, create a timeline as to when the new salespeople should be hired, trained, and deployed, so the goal of expanding into California is a reality, not just a dream to be pushed back month-by-month and never realizing the revenue projection.

Not every detail and wrinkle in the strategy is as important as others – prioritize in advance to find the most effective use of time and resources to realize the greatest result. Which of these two goals will have the greatest impact for a company, assuming they will require equal resources: (1) New and upgraded office furniture for the marketing department, or (2) hiring three new salespeople? If the answer sounds simple, ask around your office to hear other opinions and you may be surprised. If the strategy is not prioritized early, then the long-term projections (missing revenue from not hiring the salespeople) will not be met.

Another rule to keep the projection versus reality gap in check, is to acquire information from various sources by a variety of methods. Having weekly or bi-weekly meetings between managers of various departments is a start, but go one step further.

First, acquiring internal information via frequent meetings between departmental managers can fix bottlenecks that arise in interdepartmental projects, customer focused deliverables, and/or manufacturing issues (as examples). Communication is the key to keeping the team on track and to be able to address small problems before they turn larger by the quarter's end when many companies hold their meetings. In addition, creating a scorecard or matrix for weekly or bi-weekly departmental evaluations with senior leadership will immediately find if the department is not reaching their intended goal or projection, and error fixing or adjustments can be made if required. Basically, surprises are kept to a minimum without information overload.

Second, the senior managers need to know more than just the information presented by the next level of managers. Some information cannot be quantified or presented via PowerPoint, but needs to be seen, felt, and experienced and not hidden by numbers or market research. If you are the CEO of the Chicago Transit Authority's city bus agency with over one million riders per day[8], would you solely read reports on the quality of ridership by your customers, or would you like to take a few rides per week (at a minimum) to have firsthand experience and to see what others see?

Each year McDonald's executives spend time serving customers and making french fries to understand and experience how the policies, procedures, menus, and all of the other decisions they make are implemented and affect the job they ask staff to perform, or how the customer may react. Managers need to be face-to-face with the worst of the problems so they can feel and see the urgency. Reports don't characterize crime the same way a hold up does; a memo does not describe food safety issues with the same impact as suffering from a virus.

Would you ask others to do something you are not willing to do yourself? Does a seemingly benign additional step (procedure, administrative task, etc.) have an unforeseen and unintended consequence? These questions are not always answered in a report or addressed in a meeting.

Visit the front line staff of the company, whether they are the telemarketers, zoo keepers, bus drivers or pilots. The CEO's job is to sell their vision to the company, and the front line staff are to carry out their tasks and fulfill this vision – get their feedback! This information on the good, the bad, and the ugly of products, policies, and processes is invaluable. Connect, adjust to solve the found issues, and keep moving to realize the achievable projection.

The final fundamental in holding the strategy vs projection gap to a minimum is being surrounded by first-rate staff. Although it may sound obvious, it is important to determine who among your

8   American Public Transportation Association http://www.apta.com/Pages/default.aspx

staff is first-rate. Upon surveying your company's recent history and finding consistent poor choices by the same managers, they would be, by definition, bad managers. Bad managers make poor decisions, and good managers make great decisions. Determine who is who and reward the good managers appropriately to keep them with the company and enchanted to return to work the next day.

In the evaluation of the managers, go a level deeper beyond just financial results. Does the manager's team understand and internalize the strategic direction of the company? Are the managers sharing more than just tasks but also the details of how and why the company is moving in the direction it is? When all levels of the staff believe in the direction and the unified goal, their motivation is greatly increased and they can think in the long-term, not just trying for short-term results.

Avoiding Common Strategy & Implementation Mistakes

The most critical mistake a company can make is to not have an encompassing strategy. As Harry Truman once said, "No decision is the worst decision." Lack of strategy can be witnessed in governments' foreign policy, monetary policy, or clearly in taxation. It is hard to imagine or believe the taxation scheme in the United States or many other industrialized nations have a clear strategy for collecting and assigning tax rules. As of 2013 the United States Tax Code is 73,954 pages long[9]. If you are able to articulate this clear and defined strategy then perhaps you are eligible for the Nobel Prize.

However, since you are reading this concise strategy book, you have taken the first and most practical step to avoid the [potentially] tragic and common mistake of not having a strategy. Addi-

---

9   http://www.cch.com/TaxLawPileUp.pdf

tional common strategy and implementation mistakes are noted below.

Avoid just looking for the easy wins, sales, or customers just because they are easy. Think more strategically as to who would be the best customer for your products, brand, credibility, and long-term success. Sometimes the low hanging fruit could be the forbidden apple. For example, Buick has developed a reputation of a car brand for more mature (older) purchasers although the company would like future purchasers to trend younger. Re-establishing the brand will not just take new rounds of advertising and marketing, but also credibility on the street – or road. If a potential consumer only observes drivers of their parents and grandparents age behind the wheel of Buicks then the car and brand will likely not be appealing to them. Cars (or SUVs, trucks, sports cars, etc.) are not sold purely on aesthetics, functionality and/or price, but what the brand represents and, hence, as the driver of this car, what your car states about you.

Buick could pick the low hanging fruit of their current and mature driver customer base for sales of new models by marketing and advertising directly to them – but significant sales by this older crowd may lose the larger strategy of attracting first time and younger purchasers.

Common mistake number two: Allowing the written budget to be synonymous with the strategy. If there is no clear and articulated strategy that is communicated to the company staff, then the budget will represent the priorities, objectives, and allocation of resources. Of course the priorities can be interpreted differently depending on who is reading the budget, so confusion is already beginning – but that is not the sole problem.

The budget must be a living document that is active and changes with business conditions. If sales are going through the roof, shouldn't more money be put into purchasing additional raw materials to create more supply? Or, what if $5MM is spent in the first six months on a social media campaign and there are zero positive measurable results, would you want to throw good money after bad because the budget said you must?

Budgets can also be used as an excuse for poor leadership and poor decision making processes. An employee may have a brilliant idea that requires small amounts of capital investment coupled with credible significant profit potential that could 'move the needle' towards a positive direction for the entire company. How many managers would dismiss the idea for a myriad of reasons and bellow the tired saying "we don't have the budget for this." That could also mean, "We don't have the ability to think, make active decisions, or follow our own strategic principles."

Common mistake number three is confusing the goal of obtaining dominant market share with profitability. A company with a large market share may sell many items or provide numerous services, but that is not a complete equation. Achieving a great product is a proper goal, and the market share could (or should) only come after that original goal is reached. Additionally, there is a missing element of a contained cost structure that ensures a sizable gross profit from each unit sold. This concept will be addressed in subsequent chapters in greater detail.

Common mistake number four: you can't win everywhere at once. Guy Kawasaki in his book Rules for Radicals identified a frequent mistake of companies trying to be everything to everyone at all times. Of course that is impossible. For example, some companies look to generate sales in every possible channel, including through vendors, direct by company in their own retail stores and via their website, other retail stores, and independent agents simultaneously.

Returning to the earlier example of consumer electronics giant Sony's bargaining power with their vendors, imagine if Sony not only wanted Best Buy as a vendor, but also committed to opening Sony's own stores, a new direct to consumer website, hired agents to go out and sell the product, and also sold through additional wholesalers for additional distribution. Even on paper it sounds like a mess of competing with themselves and absolute over-saturation. Albeit, this is also an over-exaggeration to show the point.

The final common mistake in creating and implementing strategy found among companies both large and small is slightly controversial. Although many managers disagree, especially those who finished their medical residencies, this may have a great impact on employee morale and productivity. **Don't work too much.** Too hard is not the same thing as too much. Requiring your employees to be at their desks into the evening every night instead of with their families and pursuing other interests is not always a direct correlation to work success.

Employees, managers, everyone needs time to take a step back and look at their work without being tired or overly exhausted. Instead of the performance metrics of hours worked, change to accomplishments, for that is what really matters. Maintain office hours of **only** 9 to 5, but create internal deadlines and do not allow people to be in the office past these hours or on the weekends. In other words, eliminate the wasted time in the office and substitute it with expeditious productivity. Meetings will be shorter and fewer, nonsense will be kept to a minimum, and emails for the sake of emails can be greatly reduced.

This leadership needs to start at the top. The executive team must set the tone, otherwise it may appear to be empty words and no one will dare to test the validity of the statement. If the CEO is in his office each night and sees the office space empty outside of his door, will the CEO be upset? Who wants to take that risk? Certainly not the mid-managers who may have no issue or problem instructing their team to stay late and on the weekends.

Top executives need to set the tone and direction, and the rest of the organization will follow.

Section Summary & Conclusion

Before creating an all-encompassing strategy, it is crucial to determine the heart and soul of the company, the purpose, or the existential reason for bringing products or services to the market. Only once you know who you are can you determine the direction of the future.

Below are the fundamental concepts and actionable items presented in this Section:

1. Companies evolve through changing their products and industries over periods of years or decades.

2. To envision the organization's future, discover the meaning behind your products first. What purpose do they serve? What is your raison d'etre?

3. Your organization is not defined by your office culture, which is rarely consistent over time.

4. Create a clear and action oriented Strategic Principle to provide guidance and direction for the company.

5. If management does not set and describe the unifying goal, only personal goals that are inconsistent across the company will prevail. Don't let others define the goal.

6. The goal must be a vision that all can see, believe in, and internalize. Not esoteric or difficult to envision.

7. Upon achieving a major goal, create new horizon level goals that are achievable but yet lofty and ambitious. Avoid complacency.

8. The Mission Statement must be pithy, clear, and provide clarity on the current tasks and offerings of the organization.

9. Benchmarking against the competition leads to all compa-

nies looking and acting very similar over time.

10. Differentiate not just in products, but in the organizational structure of the company and use the system as a competitive advantage. Integration and operational effectiveness are extremely difficult to copy, dissimilar to the mimicking of specific products.

11. Evaluate your competition consistently and search for advantages and disadvantages.

12. Competitive forces shape strategy, acknowledge these concepts, and discover within your own industry how to best leverage your organization.

13. Multi-year projections must be reasonably accurate, otherwise they are easily dismissed and inaccurate predictions come with substantial consequences.

14. Recognize the common strategy and implementation mistakes so they can be avoided.

Section Two: Does Your Current Business Model Need Refinement?

"You Know Your Business Model is Broken When You're Suing Customers."

PAUL GRAHAM, ENTREPRENEUR & VENTURE CAPITALIST

In practical terms the Business Model is a roadmap of how to execute and achieve the company's long-term vision for their concept or activity – their product. There may be major hurdles and complex solutions to achieving big picture visions such as landing a man on the moon, or replacing the horse and buggy with a Ford Model T on every road in America. Achieving significant growth and/or entering into a new frontier may require a significant re-imagination of the current Business Model. This is why companies with astounding growth are often new, far from established, and do not have the heavy weight of bureaucracy and prior action and thought patterns holding them back.

In this next section, we will detail what constitutes a Business Model, and the factors to evaluate if your company needs to create a new model or should keep the existing structure to achieve the desirable growth.

Defining the Business Model

There is not an 'official' or consensus definition of a Business Model, the descriptions run from an all-encompassing combination of products, logistics, staffing, and sales & marketing to the straight forward no frill explanation of "nothing else than a representation of how an organization makes (or intends to make) money" by Peter Drucker.

Mark Johnson in **"Reinventing Your Business Model"** has developed a superb and practical Business Model definition as explained in the following paragraphs. Johnson describes the Business Model as four interconnecting areas or concepts, with the first being the most important. They are the (A) Customer Value Proposition, (B) Profit Formula, (C) Key Resources, and (D) Key Processes.

Figure 3: Business Model Concepts

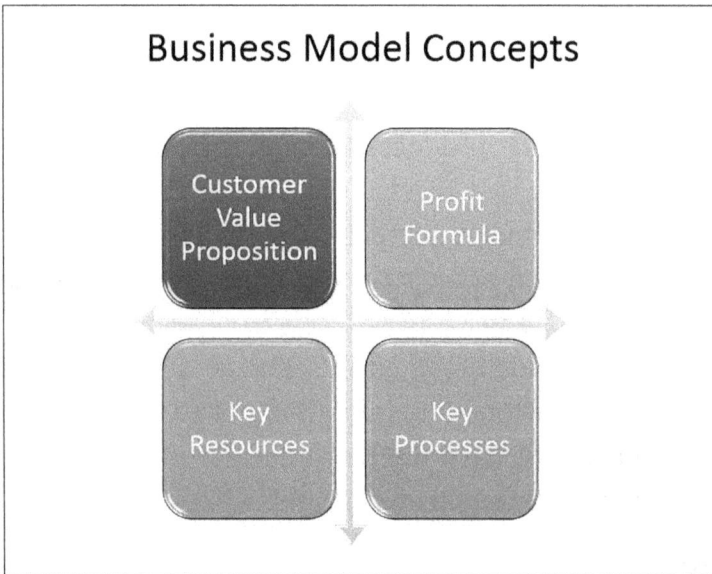

Business Model Concepts

Customer Value Proposition

Profit Formula

Key Resources

Key Processes

---

10   Adapted from 'Reinventing Your Business Model' by Mark Johnson

Simply stated, the Customer Value Proposition is how the company or organization gets the 'job' or activity completed. This could be a service, tool, or product that satisfies a need, or method or process to eliminate a pain. Basically, it is your company's core offering to consumers or society. The key is to understand all aspects of the activity to be completed so the offering can be designed in reverse with the needs of the customer in mind. Do not create a product and then search in hope of finding a customer. Find potential customers' wants and needs first, then design the product around them. This concept posits that finding success without a known and identified customer before beginning would be unlikely to result in a significant market size for the product.

However, the 'Lean Startup' model has a slightly different approach in discovering customers' wants and needs, and how to best target them. Established companies will find the customer first and then organize the operations around reaching and selling to that group; the Lean Startup begins with a few hypotheses on who the customer may be and begins to experiment to find the most efficient and productive avenue. There are multiple steps of gathering information, evaluating, and shifting or pivoting the target audience or distribution avenue towards the greatest return on investment. In other words, the company assumes it does not know exactly where to target and through an organized trial and error process will determine how to position itself.

Your Customer Value Proposition will be superior in the marketplace if the current options are non-existent, limited or poor at meeting a need. Indeed this is obvious when stated aloud, but worth noting to be very clear. Simply stated, create a better product or service based on the need that is to be solved than the existing options currently offer, or create a new one, but be sure there is a customer for this product.

The second interconnected attribute of the Business Model according to Johnson is the Profit Formula, this is "how the company creates value for itself while providing value to the customer."[11] Basically, how the company makes money for themselves and sells products by providing a sustainable reason for consumers to purchase. The Profit Formula (a model and not a mathematical formula) consists of the following inputs: the Revenue Model, Cost Structure, Margin, and the Resource Velocity. Do not be intimidated by the myriad of descriptions and subsets in creating this Business Model, each item is quite simple and creates a clear big picture in analyzing the Profit Formula.

The Revenue Model is a simple equation of the quantity of goods or services sold multiplied by the sale price. Price times volume.

The Cost Structure measures the Cost of Goods and the overhead to run the business or organization. Without a doubt there are many factors to consider in creating the Cost Structure, including property, cost of labor, economies of scale, and specialized equipment that cannot be replaced or substituted.

Margin is the amount of gross profit needed per item or unit sold to reach the company's profitability goals based on the forecasted total number of sales.

The Resource Velocity is how quickly the inventory, resources, and assets must move and turnover to reach the forecasted sales amount, and thus reach the anticipated profit. Included is the consideration of the size of staff and how many units they could or should produce in a given time period and the available or allotted capital.

The third element of the Business Model are the Key Resources; these are the people, equipment, assets, branding and technology that differentiate companies or organizations and are absolutely necessary to deliver the product or the Customer Value Proposition. Nearly every company has an accounting department, or other support staff that assists the company,

---

11   (Johnson, Christensen and Kagerman 2008)

but these departments will not create a significant value in the market that differentiates one company from another. It is rare that the purchase decision between competing companies is determined by the quality of accounts payable department for either firm. Or, would you choose between an iPhone or Samsung mobile phone based on the quality of the interns at each company?

Naturally, there are vital employees beyond just those in the leadership team. At ExxonMobil, BP, and Shell, there is a constant fight for the best geoscientists and engineers to develop a cost effective method to pull oil or natural gas out of the ground in the most inhospitable environments. There are about 50,000 employees at Google, but a team of only two people, Paul Buchheit and Sanjeev Singh, designed and created Gmail.[12]

The forth element in Johnson's Business Model definition are the Key Processes. These processes are just what you may imagine them to be: the methods to organize and manage, and to keep consistency throughout the company and the products. This could include the training process, using best practices for the sales team, manufacturing, internal culture, and the basic rules. These processes should be scalable and consistent.

These four elements are all intertwined and any significant change within one element will affect the others.

Roger is contemplating Ramicant's Business Model and if he can identify these for main elements and create a clear plan. He'll begin by asking these questions:

A. Why should someone care about our products?

B. How will we become more profitable (not how 'can,' but instead how 'will')?

C. What critical functions do we need to have in place?

---

12   (McCracken 2014)

The first question of why someone should care about your products relates to the Customer Value Proposition and the very essence of your company's offerings. Ramicant manufactures pumps, compressors, blowers, and fans that are used for oil and gas companies in the field. Since the company already has a product line he'll need to think differently than if he is searching for a new product offering for the market. Rogers asks himself: 'what activity needs to be completed that these tools will be essential in providing?'

The answer is not the specifications of the compressors, or the exact amount of air or fluid that a blower can expel, instead it is the reason why this action is executed and why your solution can perform it better than any other options available.

The second question answers the Profit Formula and the subsets within the model. At its core is the number of units needed to be sold and the price for each. Roger will factor in the costs of goods to assemble and/or manufacture the components necessary to build the products, and calculate the business' overhead. Also considered are the amount of product that needs to be sold to reach the level of success the firm envisions.

Perfecting the product offerings towards the market will be reviewed in more details in the next sections, but at this time Roger will study where the company is now without major change or adjustment.

The third question answers which processes and resources are absolutely necessary to provide and deliver a winning Customer Value Proposition. The answer is in two sections: the processes which includes training and management oversight, and the resources which focuses on the people and technology.

Focus on the activity to be completed and the resources required to achieve it. Who are the key people? What technology, train-ing, sales practices, and services needs to be in place? What fulfillment processes and duties should be altered for a better experience for the customer?

Too many questions to answer at this stage, more answers will come in the following sections.

Many of us tend to think of Business Models as tools to support for-profit corporations only, but non-profits such as charities and higher education can benefit too. Now, an introduction to the Western Governors University (WGU), an accredited online only provider of Bachelors and Masters Degrees for students living in all 50 States. The University was founded by nineteen Governors who have integrated the online degree programs with their State Universities, although concurrently financially independent.

The WGU addresses the needs of students in three areas to cre-ate a strong Customer Value Proposition. First, the $6,000 an-nual WGU tuition is very modest compared to the national aver-age in 2012 of $14,300,[13] offering a similar quality education to a traditional post-secondary school without the high overhead of a physical campus and support staff. Second, the WGU focuses on achievements in learning, not the length of time in a class-room (Profit Formula). This change of philosophy allows stu-dents to graduate faster and with lower costs through skills and competency testing. They can advance through the curriculum at their own pace. Third, WGU has a metric of success that al-leviates online learning's negative connotation of inferior quality and inability to find meaningful employment. The metric tracks the percentage of employers who rate WGU graduates as equal to or better than their counterparts who graduated from other colleges and universities. In the last available report from 2012, the metric stated a 95% rating from employers, a true success

---

13   http://nces.ed.gov/programs/digest/d12/ch_3.asp

(Key Process & Key Resource).

The Profit Formula was calculated to launch an affordable and accessible online university for those who are currently working, and/or those in rural areas without access to traditional colleges and universities.

When the Business Model Craves Change

When is it time for a great athlete to retire, or a weekend warrior to hang up the basketball shoes? Luckily, knowing when a Business Model needs to be changed is slightly less emotional. Below are three major strategic situations as outlined by Mark Johnson to be used as a guide to determine if your company needs a new model.

First, disruptive innovation is a constant due to technological improvements and creative competition. In the Oil & Gas Industry, new techniques (sometimes controversial) such as hydraulic fracturing, known as fracking, have created new drilling opportunities in areas that were previously considered obsolete or exhausted. Since the current oil price is so high, even expensive and risky exploration and production operations are welcomed in states and counties across the country. Without a doubt, fracking is not welcome in every area either by law or popular opinion, but a large market still exists with over 1.1 million wells in the United States alone.[14]

With this tremendous number of new wells coming online in locations such as Ohio, Wisconsin, and the extremely active North Dakota, new businesses are forming to service and provide support to the operations nationally. Existing operating companies are developing entirely new Business Models to manage the new technology and equipment, locations, and services and goods

---

14   http://www.fractracker.org/map/

provided by vendors such as proppants (injected material to induce fracturing treatment), to service the industry in remote locations domestically.

The second example of an occurrence that may change your existing Business Model is a refocus on a particular or specific job to be completed. For example, Emirates Airline refocused their strategy to become the world's most traveled long haul [distance] carrier with Dubai being the hub city for international flights between continents. Emirates is positioning itself and Dubai as an efficient one-stop hub to switch planes and reach most major cities in the world. For this transformation of strategy and Business Model, Emirates will need to open new routes in more cities worldwide, including nearly doubling the cities served in the United States alone. Additionally, new wide-body jets are needed to handle the increased number of passengers per flight, and to do so in comfort for intercontinental travel. Emirates purchased an additional 50 Airbus A380 superjumbo jets for a list price of $20 billion to add to their previous fleet purchase of 40 in 2013.[15]

The third strategic situation to change your Business Model is when a low cost disrupter enters your product market and creates tough competition and resets the playing field. In the case of big box retailers Lowes or Home Depot, they were able to upend the smaller, often higher margin 'mom & pop' hardware stores in Hometown, USA. These smaller and independent stores needed to either match prices, find another value to offer to the market, or go out of business. Unfortunately, many of these small stores did go out of business as they weren't able to adjust their Business Model to a winning formula in time, or didn't have the knowledge to do so.

15   http://www.bloomberg.com/news/2013-11-16/emirates-said-in-talks-to-order-50-airbus-a380-superjumbos-1-.html

Business Model Change Framework

Should you be jumping to the conclusion that your Business Model needs significant change and redevelopment, step back to analyze once more. Is the opportunity or the goal of the new plan large enough, and is the market powerful enough to take the financial and business risk? Is this a new concept or a market game changer? Your answer should be a resounding 'Yes' before remaking your entire process.

To assist in the evaluation process in determining if your company needs a new business model, consider the following questions:

1. Will the new activity have a captivating Customer Value Proposition with great confidence of its success?

2. Does the new model build a cohesive unit of the Customer Value Proposition, Key Resources, Key Procedures, and Profit Formula, all interlocking and able to support another?

3. Have you considered the effects of this new model on competitors and if it will significantly unsettle their Business Models?

Answering Yes to the above three questions is a sign that your company is ready for a Business Model change and for the next step in success.

Section Summary & Conclusion

The Business Model is the vision on how the company performs the service, or creates and sells a product. It is the action or the ambition, and the organizational method behind the company.

A strategic change of course may require a new Business Model, but carries significant risks. If your new concept or plan can answer the fundamental questions appropriately, then success is certainly achievable.

Below are the fundamental concepts and actionable items presented in this Section:

1. New business plans and strategies may require a rethinking of the current business model.

2. The business model is defined as four interlocking elements:

    a. Customer Value Proposition

    b. Value for Customer

    c. Key Resources

    d. Key Processes

3. The 'Lean Startup' approaches discovering the target market through trial and error, as opposed to pre-assuming the target market and building structure and processes around this goal.

4. The conditions that warrant Business Model change:

    a. Disruptive Innovation

    b. Refocusing on the job, service, or task to be performed

    c. Low Cost Disrupter entering the market

5. Before switching Business Models, consider the significant risk and review the framework to be confident of the likelihood of success.

Section Three: Aligning the Value Curve

"Price is What you Pay, Value is What you Get"

WARREN BUFFETT

Almost every company believes the product or service they offer is different, unique, or better priced and so it should sell in the open market. The remaining companies either don't believe they should sell product in competitive environments, or rely on a game changing factor such as powerful political influence to move the purchasing process forward. Since not everyone has a powerful friend in Washington to push sales through to you, you must compete and win. The real question is how.

For decades many business schools taught their students, undergraduates and graduate students alike, that the key to winning is differentiation, segmentation, and customization to the market. While this has been successful in various circumstances, significant future growth will reside in moving away, and in the opposite direction of segmentation and customization. Each time the market is segmented it is, by definition, a smaller pool of potential customers. Your goal must be the opposite, to attract the largest possible number of clients or customers to purchase your items.

You cannot always beat the current competition on the bench-marks the industry has chosen, but you can create a new and unique market where there is no competition and you dominate. This chapter will show you how to separate your company's offerings from the competitions, and how to create an even larger market for your goods than you are currently seeking.

Defining the Value Curve

Value innovation is the key to success. The concept is to compete on different and/or additional factors than your industry competitors, and those that your customers care most about, while concurrently attracting new customers to purchase your product who previously were uninterested or unaware. Since that is quite the long sentence and thought, we'll break it down step-by-step throughout the chapter.

The first step is building the framework so a proper evaluation of your current offerings and roadmap to future offerings can be built. W. Chan Kim and Renee Mauborgne in their book **BLUE OCEAN STRATEGY** have constructed a very valuable and elegant strategy canvas that will map the value curve as shown and described below. First, an explanation of the value curve: it is a visual representation of how a company, or industry, positions itself relative to their competition on the competitive factors that are often benchmarked. This is a relative performance indicator, and displays the inherent benchmark assumptions of how and on which factors the industry competes. The vertical axis measures the value of the offering, with high representing a comparative superior value and low being an inferior value in the marketplace.

FIGURE 4: SIMPLE VALUE CURVE

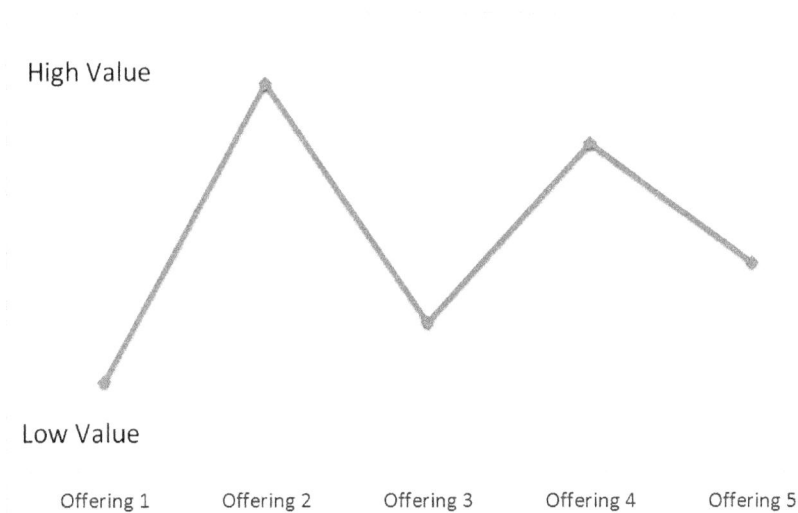

High Value

Low Value

Offering 1   Offering 2   Offering 3   Offering 4   Offering 5

For example, if your firm is selling a near commodity object such as basic residential ceiling fans (it is understood there are many factors to differentiate between models, please assume this is an entry level, low frills ceiling fan), then price is a substantial factor when choosing between models and manufacturers. For this example, let's refer to the ceiling fan model name as the Huntsman. If the Huntsman has a high price at the top of the market, then its value is low on the value curve, and near the horizontal axis. Conversely, if the Huntsman has similar benefits to the others in its class and is priced at the bottom of the market, then there is a high value and the placement is near the top of the graph. Other points on the horizontal axis which contain the often benchmarked competitive factors, could also be performance of the fan (Cubic Feet per Minute), color selection variety, ease of installation, longevity of the device, and manufacturer warranty. These are all options to judge the quality of the product and are competitive factors for consideration of which unit to purchase.

If you are shopping for a ceiling fan for your home, you may be making mental comparisons between the products, with some factors being more important than others. Keep that concept in mind for later in this chapter to discuss which competitive factors to keep, and which to reduce or eliminate.

The ranking of how the Huntsman ceiling fan compares to other ceiling fans in its class is listed below. As you can see, the Huntsman has an equal price range and a larger selection of colors offered than the industry or market as a whole, but trades in a lower reliability value.

FIGURE 5: SIMPLE VALUE CURVE

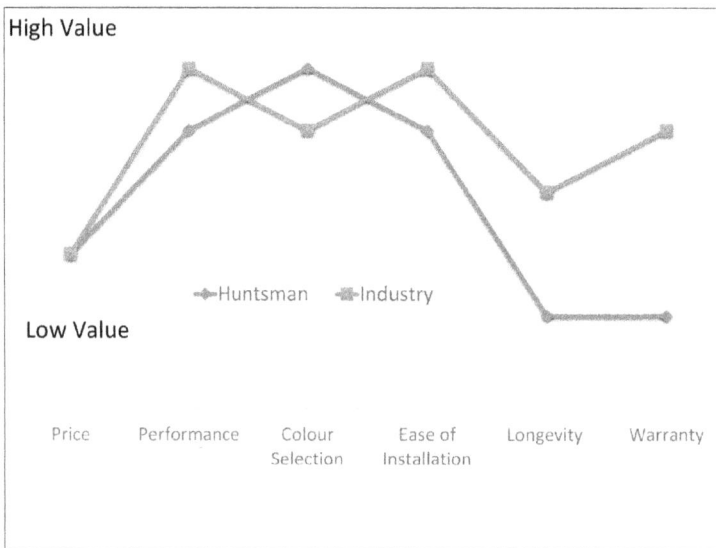

This framework can be created for any product or service within any industry, it is a tool to find how your company compares to existing competition. However, the real power of this framework is to discover where the industry and competitors are not, what your company can offer to differentiate with alternatives to set itself apart from competition to be truly unique, while simultaneously expanding your reach for more customers – not less as per segmentation.

Benchmarking: The Good, The Bad, & The Ugly

When contemplating and discovering the competitive factors or value points to plot on the horizontal axis for your own company, you may feel the tendency to list the same points your company has used to compete for years. Plainly said, these points are your industry's benchmarks.

Very often benchmarking leads to companies looking and acting alike, to the point where the products become generic. A conversion has resulted in similar products, processes, and value being offered to the customer throughout the industry. This can be magnified when companies outsource some of their services, often to the same companies to fulfill the order.

The primary goal of the value curve framework is to decide where your firm does, and does not, want to compete on the competitive factors in order to be differentiated and without competition. With benchmarking, many firms decide they want to compete on all of the common industry factors and do not think strategically outside of the current confines or market boundaries. This is where strategy leaves science and becomes an art. In the world of high finance, they refer to this as reading the "right side of the graph" referring to the equity (stock) price that is yet to be written in the future. An excellent stock trader will have an educated idea [guess] based on fundamental and/or analytical data from past performance of the future price.

Developing the right side of the graph to find more and unique competitive factors is a study of the wants and needs of your current customers, and also those who would be customers if your firm altered the offering to better fit their needs. This evolving of competitive offerings is not plausible under benchmarking, for this is an unwritten and uncharted path – the opposite of benchmarking.

The Value Curve in Practice

Step One: Where Are We Now?

Now that the theory and general concept is clear, it is time to create your strategy to offer a unique position in the market in order to greatly expand sales. There are a few additional key concepts to share, and they will be explained as we create the step-by-step guide in the following pages.

The first step in creating your organization's new strategy is to create your current value curve. It is recommended that this is performed in a team environment to gather multiple perspectives and to achieve buy-in for the final product. It is very common not to have complete agreement on which are the current competitive factors and industry benchmarks. Some of the factors you will find in future steps are slightly irrelevant and others are crucial.

In this exercise, depending on how many business managers are part of your organization's team, try dividing the group into two units, each with the same task to work concurrently and independently. Place a time limit of either sixty or ninety minutes; be aware this time limit may be perceived as either too short or too long by participants in the room. Truthfully, if there is currently a clear and defined strategy that is well communicated, then this exercise should be over in ten to fifteen minutes. This exercise is not only practical in deciding where you are today before deciding where you can go in the future, but also a test of current strategy and how it is communicated.

If your organization is multinational, or even multiregional within a large country, be conscious about where these representatives from distant offices are positioned within either group or if they represent their own group. Often overseas or distant offices perceive their challenges and business climate to be unique or more demanding, and consequently believe management in headquarters does not understand their plight or strategy. Be mindful these staff members may mention interesting or unique competitive factors to consider, or could attempt to derail the process in their favor.

Once the two groups have finished their value curves, it is time to compare and contrast to find the similarities and differences. Is the current strategy easily identifiable from the work performed and presented? If yes, does the strategy allow your company to differentiate from competitors, or is it more benchmarking and marching toward commodity pricing? If no, this exercise should prove the need for serious strategy change as illustrated by the lack of common goals and lack of differentiation in the industry or market. A picture speaks a thousand words.

Step Two: How to Find the Right Side of the Graph

Arguably, this is the most difficult and time consuming task of the entire strategic journey. The second task is to find the areas where the industry does not compete and your company can adjust the offerings to find more customers and increase sales. You will need research, imagination, and perhaps a new perspective on how to evaluate the offerings to consider not just the old benchmarks, but also to find substitute or alternative products to complete the purpose that your product serves.

Field Work

In Section One, we discussed how to fix the 'Projection versus Reality Gap' by experiencing your product, or service, and seeing it in action the way a customer would or could. This next step goes a little bit further by sending managers into the field (for at least five days) to interview and observe the customers who use the product, and also those (if possible) who use a competitors' service. Not just talk to them, that information could be gleaned from market research, go deeper. Watch the user's experience the product first hand, not what they say about it. Be sure not to be trapped into speaking only to the purchasers of the product, they are not always the people who are the users. If your firm sells power saws, the construction workers in the field are the users, and the company purchasing agent in an office is the buyer. The buyer may not tell you anything of value to make it worth your trip.

Your goal is to identify new offerings that serve the customers' wants and needs that are not currently being addressed by any other firms. Do not be constrained by what is traditional, the norms of your industry, or within your class of product (high end vs low end). Think across the industries and how other substitute products from other industries can deliver the same value or job to be performed. In a preceding chapter, it was noted that Southwest Airlines' Strategic Principle stated *"Meet customers short-haul travel needs at fares competitive with the cost of automobile travel."* This is looking across other industries to find the competing substitute. In this step, find the substitute or alternative product/service/method, and find a method to integrate it into your offering. Add a new competing factor on the value curve. Instead of dinner in a restaurant, the substitute is restaurant quality frozen food at home from the grocer.

The key information to learn is what the customer values the most, and what the customer values the least. Challenge the long accepted norms of the industry and previously perceived needs of the customer. It may be surprising, but not unusual, to find your highest internal cost competitive factor is not valued by your customer and is simply draining your resources with no strong value creation.

Discover the secondary products that are used in conjunction with your own core offering to see how they integrate, such as software utilities (application program on a tablet) or physical tools in construction (drill bits on a drill, or safety equipment attaching to tools). Could integrating any of these secondary products into your product offering be productive for the company's value creation?

Creating New Curves

Upon completion of the field research to see how the actual users of the products experience them, it is now time to draw and create new value curves. Assemble your team once again and divide into smaller groups than the first meeting; assign each group to draw at least three new curves. There is no set time limit, but provide ample time for people to be relaxed and allow all of their ideas to be heard. There should be numerous ideas of complimentary products and services that can be offered, and even some of the original factors to be expunged, or lowered. Those factors that are falling out of favor will be the topic of an upcoming section.

This is an exercise of both the information that was gathered and researched, and also the ability to think creatively and beyond the typical constructs. You and your team will need to ignore the old ideas and normal methods; the current procedures, policies and biases will all need to be pushed back. While creating the new curves and competitive factors, ask these questions:

A. Why do we operate in this way?

B. Is it appropriate today?

C. Will it be significant tomorrow?

Consistently change the question to achieve a new perspective. For example the question is not "how do we sell more nuts and bolts?" The question that should be asked is "how do we make more net profit for the company?"

Are the customers' 'pain' points clear? Go beyond just your specific product or service, if your company's product is an online 'cloud' database and the website is slow, that is a pain. Yes, consider relevant information that should be addressed in the value curve, but go deeper. What is the database product used for? Is it purely numbers and raw data that must be analyzed to be of value? Is it a database of contacts so your clients can sell their offerings to these people? If so, go a step further and investigate your client's end goal: for them to sell more. Facilitate your company's offering to match your client's **real** need.

Once the **real** need of your clients and the potential larger world of clients is recognized, work backwards from the end goal to find the services that need to be offered to match the goal. The common method of thinking is what can your company offer and where does it take us, work in the reverse and the opposite of that thought. For example, using the aforementioned concept of the database product which is purchased by clients so they can achieve more sales, take this concept and think what else do they need to make more sales? Could it be a service to create introductions, more details on each person in the database that could make a cold call more effective? Think from the end goal first.

As the new ideas are being discussed within each group, be conscious of 'group think' moving the strategic direction in one way or another. Consequently, not every idea will be enthusiastically welcomed or heard. Encourage the groups, delicately, by fighting through the dominant personalities to have multiple viewpoints. Also, in these groups, rank must be set aside. There should not be a 'boss' with multiple 'yes people.' All ideas should be considered and all should feel welcome to participate without fear of retribution.

Before presenting each of the findings, or new curves, to the group, create a label for each curve that describes the theme or overriding new concept or thought. For example, if your organization owns a group of restaurants and the new thought was the aforementioned restaurant quality frozen food sold at grocery stores, then the title of a new curve could be "Eat Out at Home 7 Days a Week."

In returning to the fictitious example of the Huntsman fan, their team researched by watching users of the fan to discover how the product could develop and meet additional needs and wants. Yes, this is a bit simplified in comparison to corporate strategy, but please allow this as an example of the theory. The users of the fans would consistently need to rise out of the chair or couch to adjust the fan speed due to changing temperatures as the sun would set during the evening, the time of day the fan was most often used. This inconvenience has been reviewed in earlier models by having a remote control, but those are not always at arms-reach as there are often an abundance of remote controls for the TV, DVR/Cable, stereo, and/or gaming systems. The product team realized Bluetooth integration may solve the problem so customers can use their phones or tablets, which are often in hand, for greater comfort.

Additionally, research suggested customers would like to have the ability to easily change the lighting fixture that attaches to the bottom of the fan. The ability to change lighting styles for new décor within their home without the hassle or expense of replacing the entire fan unit is an added value that is unique to the industry.

It also provides an opportunity to sell more products. These new competitive factors are represented in the new value curve below. It is recommended that your teams construct several value curves similar to this as indicated in the preceding paragraphs.

FIGURE 6: VALUE CURVE, TECHNOLOGY PACKAGE

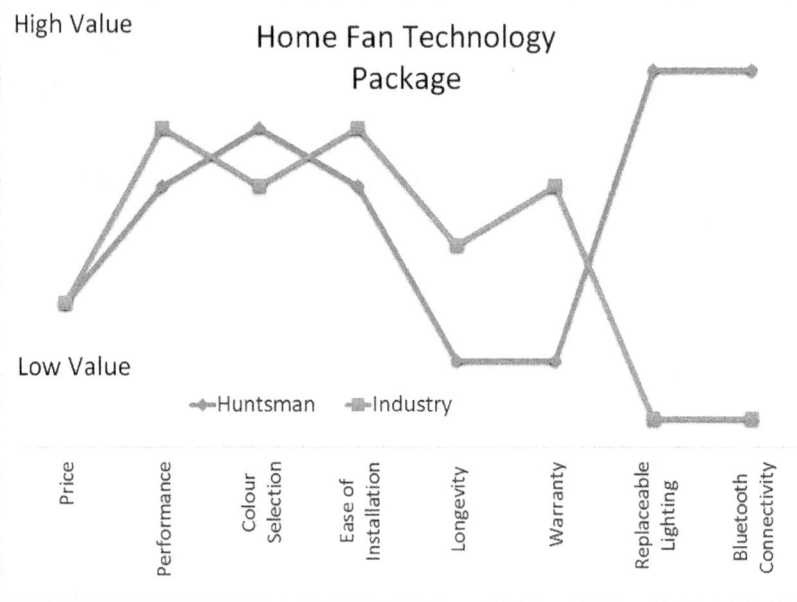

Evaluating the New Ideas

Best practices would recommend inviting your core audience of existing and potential customers, managers, and executives to judge and evaluate the new value curves to determine what ideally fits their needs and excites them. In reality, unless your company is very powerful and respected it will be quite difficult to garner this audience to listen to your proposals. The advice and suggestion is to attempt to have these core constituents come to your offices and judge via the following procedure as written by Kim & Mauborgne. Create large posters of each value curve and spend up to ten minutes to explain each. If the concept takes longer than ten minutes, then it is already too complicated and should be reworked or tossed out.

Once all of the pitches are heard, allow the judges to choose their top three to five favorites using stickers or some other open and clearly identifiable marker on the value curve poster. Having this process in the open builds confidence through transparency. Equally important is to allow the judges to explain and provide feedback on why they chose particular value curves, and did not choose others. This is invaluable, hopefully honest, feedback from your audience and customers.

If your company is not able to gather a sizeable group of judges from customers and potential customers it is perfectly acceptable to do this in-house with your management team.

This feedback from your core audience of visiting judges is another opportunity to determine which competitive factors are internally perceived to be important and are not valuable or marginal at best to the customer. Could your firm have been championing the wrong selling points? Conversely, which factors has your company been ignoring that are very important to customers that has only been recently discovered via the expanded value curve and/or additional customer feedback via judging?

If your company relies solely on focus groups or additional market research to best determine the new value curve, here is a word of caution. A focus group will only share what they know and is safe, and not often think beyond to the next step or to what is risky. The market researchers cannot test a product that is not yet available to the public, for the public is not familiar with it. The market researchers can easily test which shampoo has the best reputation, or how local theatre goers perceive the quality of the theatres. Follow all of their advice and prepare for a route of non-explosive growth.

In Guy Kawasaki's RULES FOR RADICALS, he provides this example of FedEx. What would a focus group say about a delivery service that is "150 fold more expensive than a stamp?" The focus group most likely would have turned the idea down. Or, Chrysler's Minivan was a brand new concept that was originally rejected by Ford and General Motors, before it became a phenomenal success. The minivan was ugly, yet revolutionary; which focus groups would have had the bravery to say "Yes! I love it!"

Remember, **it is not what people say, but what they do!** Your focus group might say they prefer the black wristwatch, but pick up the yellow striped wristwatch on the way out the door if the choice was given. It is brave to say what you really think, so it doesn't always happen.

Your team should now be armed with a shortlist of the new competitive factors to focus on from the top ranked or winning selection of value curves. Evaluate the complete picture or compiled list of competitive factors once again with the mindset of considering the sustainability of the product differentiation. Will the customers continually see or perceive this value? How long until competitors imitate? Will there be a large enough market and reward to take the risk and deploy resources?

FIGURE 7: IS THE DIFFERENTIATION IN THE MARKET SUSTAINABLE?

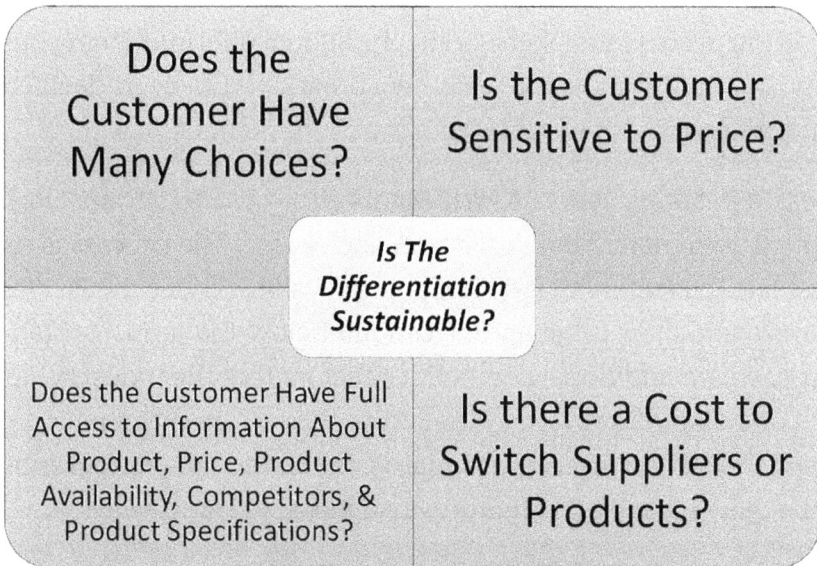

Does the Customer Have Many Choices?	Is the Customer Sensitive to Price?
Is The Differentiation Sustainable?	
Does the Customer Have Full Access to Information About Product, Price, Product Availability, Competitors, & Product Specifications?	Is there a Cost to Switch Suppliers or Products?

Making decisions is arguably the paramount role of executives at any organization, and creating expanded and new value curves is certainly a very meaningful and deliberate process that will require important choices to be made. Before moving to the next step, be mindful of the tendency for some companies to over-study and under-react or move too slowly. Essentially paralysis by analysis. If your organization has an excellent idea, move on it! Don't take too long to study and discuss or the window of opportunity may close quickly. The same may be said of a competing firm that has innovated successfully, if their new model or product is very successful then adapt internally and take advantage of this new value. Don't study the issue and talk about it until everyone's hair turns gray, be bold and take action.

Taking Action

The goal of the next step is to both simultaneously expand your potential market size by offering additional values to attract more customers and at the same time becoming more price competitive by lowering your costs. There may have been feedback earlier in the process that some of the traditional offerings from your company or the industry wide benchmarks have been deemed unnecessary or of low value from the client point of view.

To assist in taking action, Kim & Mauborgne created a framework entitled 'Eliminate, Reduce, Create, and Raise.' The process is to: eliminate the factors that do not provide value; reduce the factors that provide little value and/or can fall below the industry standards; create additional competitive factors that the industry has not competed on previously; and raise the factors that should be raised well above industry standards. Similar to the photographs in the movie 'Back to the Future,' bad ideas will fade away:

FIGURE 8: FRAMEWORK TO PERFECT VALUE CURVE

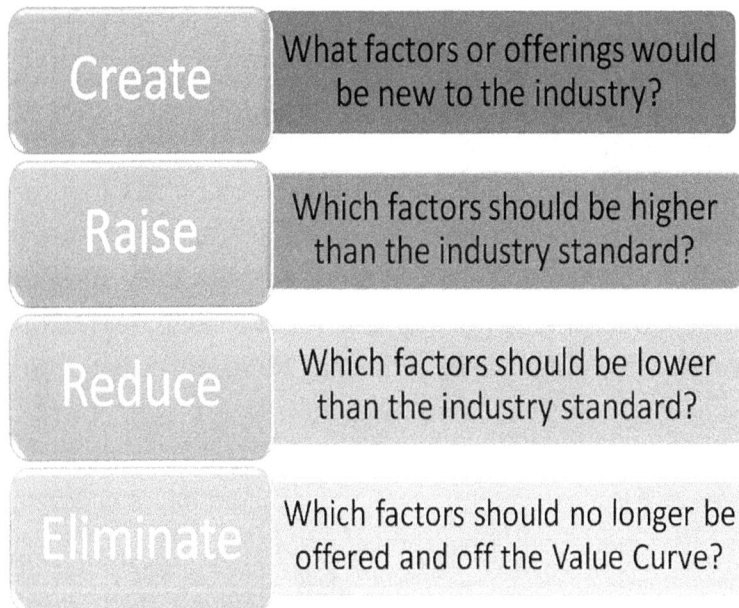

Create	What factors or offerings would be new to the industry?
Raise	Which factors should be higher than the industry standard?
Reduce	Which factors should be lower than the industry standard?
Eliminate	Which factors should no longer be offered and off the Value Curve?

This framework assists in taking action by clarifying the earlier feedback received from the value curves. **Have a specific answer for each of these for questions or categories.** Remember, the goal is to reduce your overall costs, so do not raise and create exceedingly expensive additional factors that will overshadow the costs that were eliminated and reduced.

Returning to the Huntsman fan example, a new value curve was constructed using the Create, Raise, Reduce, and Eliminate method. To be consistent with the goal of having a superior price value, the new idea of Bluetooth was eliminated as a cost concern. Items that the market does not value but the industry competes on should also be eliminated when applicable.

Second, to lower cost, the number of colors being offered to the market has been reduced. Huntsman's feedback and research found that customers largely preferred basic colors and a large selection is not a strong added value.

FIGURE 9: VALUE CURVE THREE

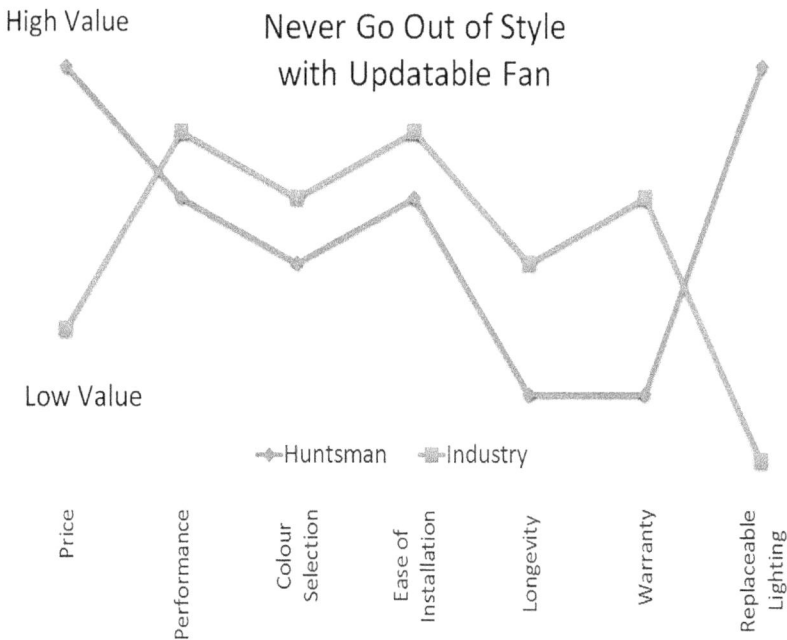

The third adjustment to the value curve for Huntsman, was to create and add the replaceable lighting fixture to the bottom of the fan. With this new configuration and value, customers are able to leave the fan installed in the ceiling, but yet change the look and feel of the room solely by modifying the easily replaceable light fixture component. New lights, new look for the room.

Finally, the raised value is the new cost. Since Huntsman will now create fewer colors and simplify the inventory and manufacturing process, they were able to differentiate their cost compared to the industry by lowering prices and hence having a higher value as denoted by the curve. They also created a new market by selling the replaceable lights.

This new value curve is entitled 'Never Go Out of Style with an Updateable Fan' due to the focus on the newly created competitive factor. Huntsman can now create new marketing materials and redirect their focus as they have a unique product offering in the market.

Who Isn't Purchasing From You & How to Attract Them

Serving and catering to only one group of customers in search of growth is extremely limiting. As mentioned earlier, business schools often teach their students to segment the market and chase a smaller subset of customers by specializing. This is not ideal and should be avoided when possible. A smaller market will equal a smaller profit potential. Segmentation is the less desirable route, widening and being more open to additional and new customers is charting the correct course.

Your sights need to be set on not just those who are your current class of customers, but also those who have not yet considered a purchase from your company or your industry by expanding on the potential laying outside your immediate or realized market. Who are the customers who could reasonably purchase your product but have not done so yet?

The concept is to find the commonality between the current customers and the non-customers, and also to think from the non-customer point of view. For example, the SUV or Sports Utility Vehicle is a combination between the pickup truck and sedan. Some car enthusiasts would also add a touch of the station wagon into the combination equation due to the practicality and aesthetics of the vehicles; the same could be said of the minivan. Not only are these vehicles very profitable to sell, but they attract new customers who want the off-road ability and safety of a large vehicle, but also the nimbleness and luxury of a sedan. Brought together, a new larger market was created by purchasers who previously only considered either a pick up or sedan, bringing in two market segments that not every automobile manufacturer catered to.

In a second example, returning to the previously discussed Western Governors University, the founders of the school wanted to attract students and provide a meaningful and valuable education that is affordable. Since the traditional market of 18 to 19 year olds who have matriculated straight from high school to undergraduate is very competitive, to attract students and to assist in completing the program once begun, WGU instead considered the needs of other segments of the population. The factors considered were age, location, employment status and type, income, and time availability. What do these non-students, or in this case, non-customers, have in common? Who are the non-customers who have considered enrolling in WGU and decided against it, and who are the customers who have never considered WGU but would like to have a higher education? What do they have in common?

In WGU's situation, these non-customers had the commonalities of small amounts of time, money, and lack of desire to spend four years on campus to earn a degree. Many of these clients were older and had families and/or jobs. WGU instead created a program

that is well below the national average in cost, and created programs that grant credits earned for real world work experience.
WGU recognized there are large numbers of potential customers
as explained in the following paragraphs, and worked in reverse
to attract and cater towards them. The first step is to understand
who the three groups are:

The potential customers fall into three distinct categories, the
Reluctant, the Unwilling, and the Unfamiliar. The first and small-
est class of potential customers are the Reluctant group, those
who purchase selectively and without consistency. They do not
have a vested interest in the market or industry they purchase
from because the value that is being offered isn't of core concern
for them. However, if the value being offered fit better with their
needs, they would be enthusiastic purchasers and would do so
with greater regularity. In simple terms, think of how often you
or your family frequents a restaurant genre? Do you only eat Thai
food once or twice a year? If so, you would fall under the Reluctant category.

THREE TIERS OF CUSTOMERS

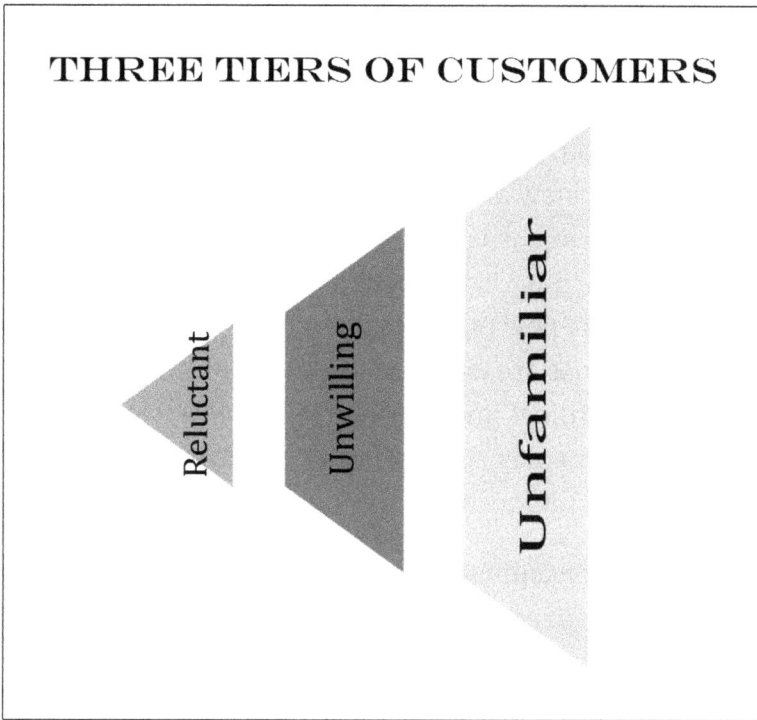

FIGURE 10: THREE TIERS OF CUSTOMERS, FIND THE COMMONALITIES BETWEEN THE THREE GROUPS

The second group of potential customers is a larger group yet further away from potential sales due to disinterest in the industry's product offerings. Naturally, this group is referred to as the Unwilling, short for the unwilling purchasers. They are familiar with the values being offered, but yet do not have the interest to follow through to a purchase or sale. For example, your firm may receive many offers from telecommunication companies to switch from a traditional phone network to an all-digital VOIP. You may be well aware of this system and offer, but do not have an interest and are refusing to switch.

Lastly, the largest of the potential customer purchase groups is referred to as the Unfamiliar. This group represents those who are unknowing or unfamiliar with the industry's offering and have not previously considered a purchase though it is plausible it could be of benefit. In the Oil & Gas industry there is a constant churn of new technology for deeper and more efficient exploration and production, such as more powerful geo-modeling software programs, or new automated drilling equipment. Since the industry is unique and is largely driven by risk aversion and not "savings" per well, it is very difficult to be given the opportunity to show the value of new products to the corporate decision makers, as their priorities are not aligned with your product offering. Lower cost or marginal improvements do not move the needle. The industry majors may be interested if they are familiar, but as a choice they are Unknowing.

The core of the conceptual framework is to discover why each of these three groups are not interested in your product. What do these three groups have in common? What need or want do these three groups have that you, or the industry, is not providing? Once discovered, think backwards from the customer point of view to how to package and implement this need into a product.

In 2002 and 2003, McDonalds studied their three groups of non-customers and concluded the commonality was not one of the traditional benchmarking standards of speed of service or general locational and/or efficiency convenience that kept non-customers from visiting their stores, but instead two major items: overall food quality, and healthy options. Once recognized, McDonalds made significant changes to their menu by using higher quality meats for their burgers and chicken nuggets, and also adding new items such as salads, wraps, and lower calorie meals. The new campaign was entitled "I'm Lovin' It" and started simultaneously in more than 100 countries.

Although these changes may sound obvious in hindsight, this was a major institutional change both in operations and mindset for the management. McDonalds is arguably the most dominant chain restaurant in the world, for it to have recognized it is in need of significant change and then expeditious execution is an exceptional accomplishment.

Section Summary & Conclusion

Segmentation and benchmarking against the industry and competition will only win small victories in a smaller market. Significant growth is achieved by expanding to reach a larger pool of potential customers, not smaller, and to distinguish the product from the competition by introducing new competitive factors. This is the value innovation.

Below are the fundamental concepts and actionable items presented in this Section:

1. You cannot always outperform the industry, but you can create a market where there is no competition.

2. Define your company's offerings as a value curve on the strategy canvas, created through team exercises.

3. Compare and contrast to the industry's offerings.

4. Discover where the competitors are not competing and what unique offerings may be created.

5. Through in-person research and interviews, determine how the product is actually used and what the customer values most, and values least.

6. What are the real needs of the customer, think from their end goal and work backwards.

7. Determine if the differentiation in the market is sustainable.

8. Not only must the product best match the customers' real needs, but it should also be a low cost product or service to reach the largest possible potential market.

9. Create, Raise, Reduce, Eliminate.

10. Recognize and define the three tiers of customers.

11. Think critically outside of the normal industry benchmarks.

12. Find the commonalities between them and develop the offerings to attract all three tiers.

13. Like McDonalds, execute quickly.

Section Four: Implementation & Buy-in

"Deep and sustainable change...requires changes in behavior among those who do not welcome the change."

DOUGLAS B. REEVES, AUTHOR

Now that the strategy has been outlined and created, how does it come into practice? The implementation answer is to successfully sell the vision to your company and for the staff to go beyond understanding the strategy, to the level of believing and internalizing. A new strategy can be a tremendous motivator in putting an end to the status quo and in reaching for the stars with a new all-encompassing vision. However, the staff must have as much faith in the vision as you do.

Not Just Hearing, But Believing: Achieving Buy-in

Chicken or the egg? Seinfeld or Friends? Strategy or Execution? The answer to all of these is the same, both. An exceptional strategy without meaningful execution is almost equivalent to not having any strategy. Practically speaking, this question of strategy or execution should never arise in a company meeting and not deploying appropriate resources and time into strategy and execution, as if that would be an option, would be ludicrous. The answer is obvious, you need both.

The first step to achieving company-wide buy-in is to include many people in the process early. Allow their voices to be heard and listened to with respect, without being dismissed immediately or entirely. A growing software company based in Utah involved multiple levels of management by assigning each team a specific area to coordinate and plan. The senior executives formulated the internal business processes and cross-departmental coordination, the mid-level managers developed the revenue, financial, and customer objectives. This broad alliance included the perspectives of many areas of expertise and varying degrees of industry experience to form an all-inclusive strategy. This helped create a cohesive plan.

Regardless of rank or experience, there can be valuable input from all sectors that is not readily apparent to management. Relying on a top down strategy without proper two-way communication is a recipe for disaster, it simply won't work. Creating buy-in is not a post strategy endeavor, but a step-by-step process that begins at the conception and formulation of the strategy itself.

The front line may not be involved in the larger picture daily, but they do see details and customer responses. Allowing early feedback and recommendations on creating the plan will provide ownership to those who were involved. When people are allowed to contribute to a plan or strategy, they'll be less likely to be negative and inhibit execution.

However, if you make the mistake of not treating your staff as though they are valued members of a team, and their contributions are not valued, they will be much more likely to be a counter to your plans or to delay implementation. Do not allow those who want to help to be entirely outsiders looking in, for they won't be on your team when you need them the most. People in general seek recognition of their work and efforts; money is not always the top motivator, public recognition of exceptional work can be equally rewarding. Of course, both are ideal.

The second step for successful implementation is the education and clarification phase. The entire company must understand how, why, when the change is coming, what this means for the company, and what it means for them as individuals. When establishing the company goals, share the vision with everyone; it is meant to be a strategic motivator that moves the organization in an upward and unified direction. Communicate relentlessly and with purpose to be sure everyone understands and eventually internalizes through repetition and clarification.

There are multiple levels of information to share with each employee as illustrated in the following model. Beginning with the company-wide goals and direction that were discussed in Section One, the Core Ideology, Mission Statement, Strategic Vision, and the Strategic Goals, this 10,000 foot view of the company will explain why the organization exists, where the company wants to be, and how it will get there.

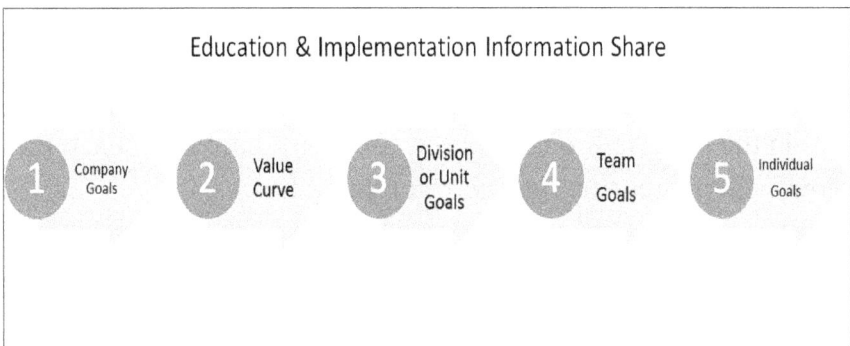

Education & Implementation Information Share

1 Company Goals   2 Value Curve   3 Division or Unit Goals   4 Team Goals   5 Individual Goals

FIGURE 11: STRATEGY EDUCATION METHODOLOGY

Next, share the old and the new value curves by explaining the purpose and the meaning behind them. In order to achieve the vision in the future, strategic change is necessary and this is the instrument on which to base future company positions and offerings.

Strategic Scorecard & Incentives

The third step is to explain the goal for your division or unit and, equally important, how you are going to achieve it. These must be clear and concise steps. Explain why each step is necessary. The critical secret to execution is for all staff to know, and truly understand, what they are responsible for and who is responsible for which decision. This can be achieved by generating a personalized scorecard similar to the following illustration and presenting it to each member of your staff. The scorecard must highlight not only the company and division goals, but list a few of the specific goals and tasks for each person. This scorecard is a constant reminder of what they're working towards in the big picture, the divisional goals, and their responsibilities. It is also a personal reminder of what each individual's goals and tasks are so there is no ambiguity as to their role and what they need to do to help the company move forward. Many strategies get lost in translation and lack of understanding as to where individuals fit within the plan. This personalized scorecard handed to each employee eliminates this common stumbling block.

FIGURE 12: STRATEGIC SCORECARD

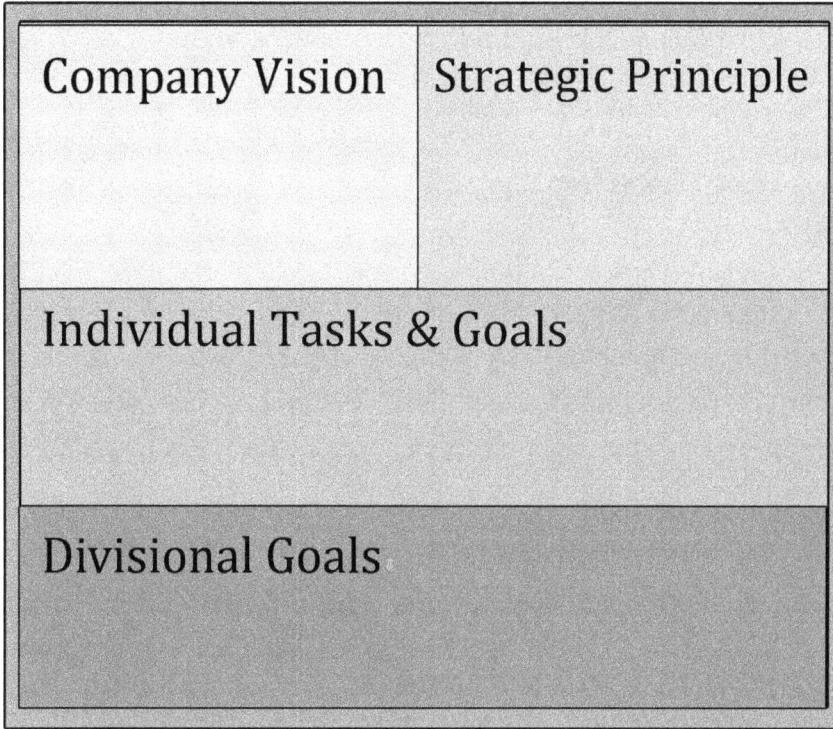

Company Vision	Strategic Principle
Individual Tasks & Goals	
Divisional Goals	

For example, in creating the scorecard for members of the sales team, the listed individual tasks and goals may be 50 phone calls a day to equal 30 sales per year per person. A staff member in manufacturing may list <1% error rate and a production increase of 10% per year. Managers should work with staff to establish challenging yet achievable individual goals.

By inserting the critical success factors into individuals' scorecard, actions will be focused on reaching the strategized results, but only if they are incentivized to do so. Knowledge of what is expected, plus accountability and incentives, whether they are positive or negative, compels people to reach to complete their task. There are many methods to provide incentives, they range from recognition, promotion, remuneration and, not least of all, fear.

An entire book, and many have, can be dedicated to the multiple methods of how to properly incentive staff. However, this concise 'how to' book, will keep it pithy, pragmatic, and useful.

Motivating Towards Execution

The simplest method of motivation is remuneration or compensation by creating or aligning bonuses with the completion or fulfillment of the assigned tasks or goals. Although there can be many goals or tasks included in a bonus scheme, an effective plan will weight the critical achievements to encourage employees to concentrate on specific areas to win the highest financial reward.

Motivate your employees by believing in them. Your employees need to want to come to work to be truly effective, or at least for them to operate at full capacity. An energized employee is a motivated employee who will go the extra mile without asking or thinking twice about it. In sports, a "weight room guy" is the player who doesn't watch the clock while in the gym in order to do the minimum recommended (required) weight lifting and leave, but instead has a passion and internalizes the needs and purpose of the work. This player will stay in the gym far beyond what his coaches ask and achieves his/her desired results on the field during games because of their extra effort. The other extreme is the "clock watcher," this player will arrive exactly on time, and leave exactly on time. They will do the exact workout plan provided (and required) to keep their coach happy, but no more and no less. This player understands why the weight room is important but does not care enough to believe in the workouts.

Who do you want on your team, the "weight room guy" or the "clock watcher"?

Your employees are members of your team, business or sports

– it is often the same. During recruitment the message towards applicants needs to be "We Want You to Work Here!" and not the corporate arrogance of selectivity and it would be your honor for us to allow you to be in our presence. By all means your company should be selective, but communicate positively towards applicants and the future work force. The best candidates will want to work for you. Let them feel appreciated and welcomed, and they will often reflect the same respect towards you. You will not always know whom the exceptional talent is or will be, but you already know you need to keep the best. If you're lucky enough to recruit highly talented people, charm them into staying for years to come. Just because your star, or average employee comes into work on Friday morning, there is no guarantee that they will come into the office on the following Monday.

When you've encouraged and charmed your employees, including the "weight room guy" and others on staff, they will reciprocate your goodwill and want to do what is best for the company and the greater good. To be truly effective employees will also need another tool, enablement. Staff should be enabled to make decisions, take responsibility, and see actions through to the end to help a customer. If this sounds implausible to implement at your company, consider the situation in basic terms: **your staff cannot fully help your customer.** Consider the long-term consequence of such an arrangement and put yourself in the shoes of the customer if an issue does arise and the customer needs assistance. So where would you rather concentrate the power? On a doer who can help customers daily and immediately, or a manager who cannot leverage his time fast enough? The organization cannot be in constant fear of the front line staff making poor decisions when dealing with customers. If an employee or manager consistently makes poor decisions, then you should evaluate why they are your employee, and not why a person in that position has been given the power to make decisions.

Believe employees will make the right decisions, give them the strength and confidence by enabling them to make decisions and act on behalf of the company. This will result in a motivated employee who will follow your strategy and vision.

Accountability & Expectations

Expectations and accountability go hand in hand, both are essential, and both must be clear before executing a new strategy. The strategy graveyard is full of plans that did not identify and specify where one person's accountability ended, and the next person's began. Setting up clear lines and providing authority for the manager to make decisions within those guidelines is crucial. After all, would you like to be held responsible for every driver in your city? Of course not, you have no control or method to hold anyone else accountable. What is the purpose of responsibility without the power to make decisions that affect the outcome? Set clear lines of responsibility for your managers, segments, and team leaders. The team leaders can again delegate further to the staff to successfully reach the goals.

Along with the power to make decisions to affect the areas for which each manager is responsible, information must be flowing and readily available. Bottlenecks of information should be recognized early and fixed accordingly. For example, line managers in Seoul, South Korea and Bangkok, Thailand may be reporting sales and production statistics to the corporate office in Virginia, which would then redistribute the data and information to the unit manager responsible for the Asia-Pacific region based in Hong Kong. The unit manager likely has responsibility over these locations and the power to make decisions, but information does not flow fast enough and needs to overcome a corporate and intercontinental bottleneck.

The Strategic Scorecard presented earlier in this section provides clear tasks and goals for each member of a team. Additionally, it also provides the expectations and the basis of how the employee will be evaluated. State the exact goals to be achieved, and the consequences if they are not met. Presenting and being explicitly clear with accountability and responsibility metrics used to evaluate employees will earn trust and buy-in for the strategy and program being executed.

Employees need to understand why achieving buy-in (and execution) is so important and the company-wide consequences if there is failure in implementation. After the Deepwater Horizon debacle in the Gulf of Mexico where a BP rig operated by Halliburton and Transocean exploded killing eleven people and released millions of barrels of crude oil onto the Gulf floor for weeks, BP and other oil & gas companies changed their strategies to be safety forward and conscious firms. If the companies had not successfully changed by buying into their new operating culture, there were tremendous risks, possibly beginning with crew members' lives. Additionally, the companies' ability to operate could have been jeopardized by increased scrutiny by regulators, difficulty in obtaining licenses and permits to operate, attracting and hiring the most talented employees, and the ability to raise operating funds in the capital markets by activist investors working to reduce value in the firm. Coupled together, these are threats to the company. If the company staff did not buy-in to the company culture change strategy, BP and other oil and gas companies, could have faced serious threats to their existences.

Internal Politics

Communication within a company, or communication within a city, state, or country will always require politicking to deliver the message and have people listen. Politicking involves two pillars, the first is creating a unified message by convincing leadership to support one plan over another, and the second is positioning the unified message to be believable, actionable, and able to overcome common hurdles.

In most groups, whether they are a small volunteer group who appreciates astronomy, or a large group of senior managers, personality differences will appear. There will be some who will want your project to fail, or succeed, solely because it is not their idea (or because it is yours) and not on the merits of the proposal. For the strategy to be built and for it to succeed, it will be necessary to build a coalition and be prepared for the sometimes inevitable fight.

Before creating proposals, research what the likely opposition will use to counter. What numbers, concepts, or questions will they argue against your idea? Know the objection and the answer before going in and head off the questions before they are asked.

In Congress, the Whip is the vote counter who will twist arms and make deals before a bill heads to the floor for a vote, the final vote count should be known before voting even begins. Very rarely is the Whip the author or the sponsor of the legislation, but instead is a member of the party leadership whose job is to follow the Speaker or the Majority Leaders legislative priorities in building a coalition behind a bill. Create an internal Whip who will do the dirty work of behind closed doors negotiations or horse-trading to see your priorities moved forward. The Whip will also recognize who has the most to lose and would consequently put up the largest fight. This information up front will be invaluable to head off internal challenges to your new strategy proposals.

Common Hurdles

This section has discussed how and what information should be communicated from management to staff to implement strategy change to best achieve buy-in and execution. Going one step further, management should identify the common hurdles and roadblocks ahead so that they can be avoided.

Not every organization or person will identify with each of these stages or have hurdles, but it is common to have varying degrees of a few or more of each. Initially recognizing these sources of resistance will assist in deployment and reduce the challenge of implementation.

The first hurdle is to convince staff that there is a need for change, to overcome the 'Status Quo Mindset.' In the case of Deepwater Horizon, not everyone at BP immediately saw a tremendous need to revamp the safety and operating culture. The thought process was, 'we operate in dozens of countries and one mistake or incident does not define a company or culture.' Management needed to convince staff that business as usual was not going to be acceptable and the mindset had to be changed. The status quo did not work and change was a must.

The second hurdle has been discussed in this section and the first section of this book, how do you inspire staff to want to approach their work differently, or to be excited about their company? This 'Inspirational Jump' starts at the beginning. What is the big picture vision of the company? Is there a 'land on the moon in ten years' inspirational vision for the organization? If yes, has the message been communicated effectively, and/or, are the staff members interested in the future of the company? If someone truly doesn't care about the company and cannot be motivated, then their priorities are elsewhere and they should not be a member of the team going forward.

The third hurdle is the 'Risk & Reward Hurdle.' Who wants to be the person who jumps up too early and champions a losing idea or movement? Fads and fashion come and go, as do strategies and those who champion them. The mid-manager who is not the author or the leader of the new strategy and is asked for support will often be reluctant to lend their name to new endeavors out of risk. What do they gain, what do they lose? Will they be compensated more if they jump in and the new strategy works? Conversely, if the new strategy fails, will they be escorted to the parking lot holding a cardboard box? What is the risk and reward for managers who have the ability to maintain the status quo and not jump in with two feet? Consider your staff member's perspectives when implementing, it may be very different than your own.

An army can only advance as far as the supply line can follow. A strategy can only be implemented as far as the resources of capital, talent, and infrastructure are deployed. The 'Deployment Game' is the fourth hurdle; managers need to be allotted the appropriate resources to execute the strategy. What good is a magnificent $1MM tool but no factory to place it in? Or what a beautiful view, but not enough funds to install plumbing. Resource scarcity can be a political game or exercise to ensure a planned endeavor falters. This occurs in Congress, the House of Commons, or any corporation on earth. As long as you are aware of the 'Deployment Game' before it occurs, you will be able to defend your plan and prepare for possible battles ahead.

Teamwork for Maximum Effectiveness

For a company to run at full speed on all cylinders, information is the fuel to power the engine. Should the fuel be too thin the engine would run sluggishly and not reach its operating potential. Conversely, when the information is too thick and/or the quality is low (meaning an overload of data and non-useful intelligence), then the engine also suffers and does not reach maximum performance. Beyond the common communication of market intelligence and financial results, sharing best practices across divisions, units, or geography is the fuel for a company to move forward and avoid common mistakes and hurdles. Memos and emails are not enough for large corporations to gain the information and experience across organizational boundaries. Instead, share managers for long-term assignments around the company and across divisions. This is an opportunity to develop managers well versed in the company's operations outside of their immediate division or traditional field of expertise. Allow managers to lose their internal biases through expanding their knowledge base and learning more about the organization as a whole.

Creating the best team naturally begins with hiring and retaining the finest people. Think about your staff now, do you have confidence in their abilities, perseverance, and personalities? Here is a simple test to gauge your fondness for your team members adapted from Guy Kawasaki[16]: If you were out with your family on Saturday morning and you saw a member of your team across the street, would you:

A. Hide in the bushes

B. Meander in their vicinity to see if you could make eye contact, or

C. Excitedly run across the street and say hello!

If you haven't answered 'C' for each member of your staff, you should evaluate why they are a part of your team. When hiring new people into your organization also consider this test, beyond their abilities are you comfortable with their persona and demeanor? Would you want to work with them in the long-term, and can you draw inspiration from your team members as well as lead them?

---

16   (Kawasaki, Rules for Revolutionaries: The Capitalist Manifesto for Creating and Marketing New Products and Services 2000)

If you didn't respect your staff member you would not run over and say hello, and if you do not respect them they should not be on your staff.

An uncommon method to organize your team is to appoint one person to be the naysayer, or the Devil's Advocate. That person's role will be to find reasons why a project or an idea should not move forward and to try to flush out the potential stumbling blocks. If this person's clearly stated role is to be this contrarian figure there is likely to be less personal resentment for the necessary negativity imposed on someone's new idea.

There may also be a safe figure to whom employees could address concerns about an upcoming product launch, or any perceived technical issues. If General Motors had designed a program of this nature before producing faulty ignition switches in certain vehicles in the 2014 recall, it may have saved a few lives and a $1.2 billion cost to administer recalls and victim compensation.

By creating a competitive environment and being open to criticism, ideas and execution should be raised above their normal standards to reach greater goals.

To go one step further in reducing risk on a product or service launch before it occurs, have your team assume the project failed and begin analysis on why. Have the foresight to view in hindsight. What went wrong? Identify the likely or potential problems before they occur and the product or project will be stronger once it actually debuts. Since there are no 'actual' problems and the project has not failed, the stress levels should be significantly lower so the team can think and act creatively to solve potential problems.

Earlier in the section, the Strategic Scorecard was introduced to distribute to your staff to share the company, division, unit/team, and individual goals. This is an excellent tool to communicate strategy and the individual big picture actions or accomplishments to reach. To continue the transition of strategy theory to specific practice and execution, use a checklist. This reframes the conversation from 'theory' to 'action.' A checklist, almost by defi-nition, lists all of the actionable tasks for staff members or teams to accomplish.

Creating team checklists will communicate what and how items are to be completed. Like almost everything else, the checklist should be pithy and concise so it is easy to follow and understand.

Multi-Disciplinary Teams

By organizing employees in multi-disciplinary teams, information will be shared across the traditional divisional borders and some of the larger picture strategy can be seen for each unit. Many em-ployees in sales know the cost to generate new business, whether that is the time and cost in the sales cycle and funnel, marketing costs, or the generic cost of goods. Teaming with members in the accounting or fulfillment departments will expose sales people to additional costs and risks they may not see, such as time to inter-nally set up new accounts, fulfillment, or risk of non-payments, etc. This type of internal information is useful to understand what type of clients would be best for the company, whether they are deeper within existing clients, or to spread as wide of a net as possible to build additional revenue streams. More information to employees leads to their seeing and believing in the larger strat-egy picture.

Procter & Gamble (P&G) used this internal method of organiza-tion and augmented it as a client and sales tool. P&G integrated people from manufacturing, logistics, marketing, finance, IT, and human resources into a customer team to ensure integration with their most valued and largest clients. P&G wanted to go deeper into companies, and not spread wider to new distributors, so they devised a strategy to achieve both their client's goals and their own sales goals.

Through integrating with giant retailers such as Target and

Walmart, P&G's task was to comprehend the customer so well that they could work jointly in developing and implementing mutual business goals and shared action plans. For example, P&G's marketing teams would study how shoppers at their client stores would browse products and make decisions to purchase. Based upon the research and recommendations, same stores sales of P&G products would increase and everyone wins. Additionally, the supply chain team would study how to increase expediency and reduce costs by working together.

A.G. Lafley, the CEO of P&G describes this win for the retailer/distributor and the win for P&G as "joint value creation." More sales for both companies, lower cost to do business, and long-term client integration all due to strategic teamwork.

Fixing the Decision Making Bottleneck

As has been mentioned numerous times in the preceding chapters, decisions are vital and may need to be made resolutely and quickly. The most effective organizations make the best decisions, and the most consistent decisions. Reaching for a consensus is often a magnificent waste of effort and, most of all, time. Instead of laboring to find a political answer that is scaled back and the lowest common denominator to all in the process, seek buy-in on the concept and the details. The following subsection will discuss how, and why.

Within your organization, is it common to find decision making logjams due to lack of accountability, authority, availability, or interest? Very often the lines of authority are blurred or mixed by separate lines of accountability. It is possible and not altogether uncommon for a unit manager to be responsible for a specific territory, but not have the authority to make decisions to govern their affairs.

If an expensive and significant piece of equipment needs to be purchased immediately for time sensitive work in the field, who is responsible for approval? This type of bottleneck often occurs at the national or global versus state or regional managerial level, or within exterior versus interior players as in the case of subcontractors or business partners.

Decisions need to be made in advance as to how much power and authority is to be placed on far away divisions of a company. If a Canadian restaurant chain is operating less than ten company owned outlets in Malaysia, could the Malaysian country manager add local flavors and ingredients to cater to their customers, or does this decision need to come out of the Canadian corporate headquarters? If the decision is to be made in the HQ, how many approvals are needed, how long does it take?

In other words, how much leeway can be granted to each unit to make decisions based upon their market conditions including branding, pricing, marketing, and product variations? Has this decision already been made on how much control or autonomy is passed, and is it assumed that it is clear to everyone?

Although the headquarters and executives can see the big picture of various business units and locations, they are not on the front line to view the individual markets and the instant client feedback. Headquarters and management will want to study recommendations and the various contributing market conditions to make smart or reduced risk decisions, but this can take a tremendous amount of time and, in effect, create a bottleneck due to numerous reasons. In some situations, no one is accountable, or too many people are accountable and the power is fought over without producing a clear and effective decision. In other cases, a decision has been made and there are too many people with veto power who kill ideas so no further progress occurs. Too much information or data is also a common sticking point for decisions; it can be an impossibly daunting task if the mountain of paperwork rises above the clouds.

How to unclog the bottleneck and ensure a clear decision making process?

The first step is to create and define clear roles and responsibilities for everyone in the management team. Of paramount importance is determining who has the ability and responsibility to make decisions. Also included down to the micro scale are the rules for business units or divisions on how much movement they can make with pricing and local advertising, and the trust to make adjustments to the brand in their local markets. If you asked multiple divisions within your company who is responsible for deciding the standard features of the next product, how many would assume it is their unit and not another? Clarification on this decision making process, among all others, will greatly reduce friction and speed efficiency.

The second step is to clarify the proposal by gathering all of the applicable information and data so a decision can be made. While gathering details, obtain opinions and feedback from the people who have front line knowledge for they will most likely be a part of the implementation of any decision, or strategy that needs to move forward. Their feedback is a major step in achieving their needed buy-in for whichever strategy is chosen.

Next, identify the people who have power to deny any decision or to veto the forthcoming strategy due to legal, manufacturing constraints, or whim. Also, identify the units that may or will be affected by the scope of the decision. Discuss and obtain their feedback for they have the crucial power to stop the project, and their buy-in will be needed. Approaching them early will make great strides in obtaining their approval.

Who the decision maker is should have already been established, and their job is to now make the decision, have the ability to move the resources into action, and be accountable for the results.

Once the decision is made, it should rarely be second-guessed. The key is to assign the people and give them the authority to make and carry out their decisions, not to cut them off at the knees to prevent them from carrying out their ideas. Notice decision by committee was not mentioned for it rarely works and only takes more time. Assign, and delegate. Someone specific is accountable and that should be the decision maker, not an entire group where responsibility is passed faster than the Kentucky Derby but no one ever wins.

Principles to Making Good Decisions Quickly & Effectively

Paul Rogers and Marcia Blenko[17] have constructed a set of standards to ensure a sound decision making process in their article, 'Who Has the D?' The following concepts are adapted from their article and are illustrated in the following infographic.

The first principle of making excellent decisions quickly and effectively are to recognize not all questions or decisions to be made are of equal importance. Some are clearly more vital than others and time should be properly allotted for evaluation and decision. Prioritizing for the decisions that generate the most impact and value for the organization is a must.

---

17   (Rogers and Blenko 2006)

FIGURE 13: EFFECTIVE DECISION MAKING

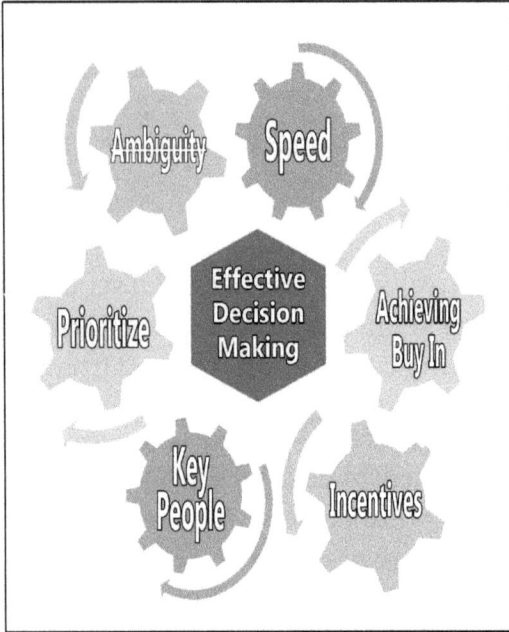

The second principle to make superb decisions quickly concern the people resources; the right people need to have their skills and abilities matched to be effective at the appropriate level and consulted when appropriate. The people information resource could extend from the senior managers to entry-level juniors, whomever has the necessary information to make the best decisions.

Do not overlook or neglect that speed counts! Paralysis by analysis is a real thing, and happens not only at large corporations overflowing with bureaucratic red tape, but also small mom & pop firms. Nimbleness is the result of quick and fast decision making, there is no other way to produce this desired capability. When quick decision making occurs on a regular basis the employees of a firm begin to notice, and the culture changes for the better. An atmosphere of an expectation to move quickly and effectively will be the norm, not the exception. Positivity moves quickly and is infectious, and quick decision making is the beginning of productivity.

Ambiguity is great when your goal is to avoid doing a task, such as assigning who is responsible for mowing the lawn, you or the home owner's association? Or ambiguity is fantastic when the written law may or may not allow a certain type of tax strategy, or real estate development in a district or zone. Ambiguity is what lawyers dream and smile about when they sleep at night. However, ambiguity in a decision making model is a nightmare. Avoid it, make certain who is accountable for what, and provide the tools and resources they need to fulfill their mission. It cannot be ambiguous who the decision maker is, who the executer is, and who is responsible for each stage of the execution.

Incentives speak louder than words, and incentives make people rise out of bed in the morning. Talk can be brilliant and effective to various degrees, but to really motivate staff to move in the right direction provide incentives and disincentives through accountability and consequence. The decision making process must involve incentives to be effective and enduring.

The final principle for effective decision making are achieving strategy buy-in by asking for assistance and feedback from those who will be executing and implementing the plan, as has been discussed at length previously. Requesting feedback and opinions early by staff members will significantly assist in creating buy-in on the strategy upon completion and execution.

Framework to Evaluate Decision Making History

To know where you want to go, it is important to first know where you have been. If your personal or organizational goal is to formulate better and faster decisions, then it is worth reviewing your prior history to find a baseline from which to measure improvement. Additionally, the following framework below could serve as a guide to supplement your current decision making process.

FIGURE 14: FRAMEWORK TO EVALUATE PREVIOUS DECISION MAKING

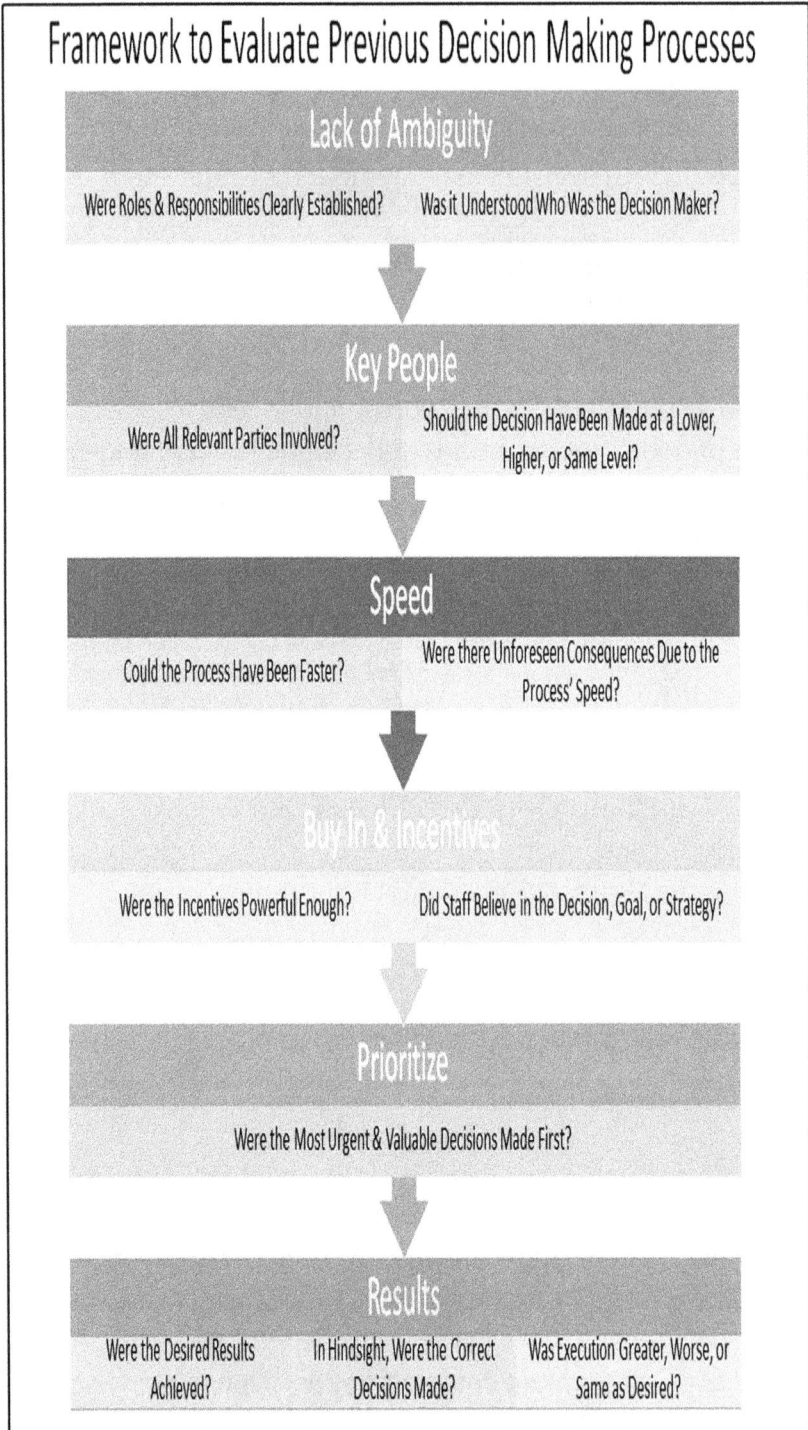

Framework to Evaluate Previous Decision Making Processes

Lack of Ambiguity

Were Roles & Responsibilities Clearly Established?   Was it Understood Who Was the Decision Maker?

Key People

Were All Relevant Parties Involved?   Should the Decision Have Been Made at a Lower, Higher, or Same Level?

Speed

Could the Process Have Been Faster?   Were there Unforeseen Consequences Due to the Process' Speed?

Buy In & Incentives

Were the Incentives Powerful Enough?   Did Staff Believe in the Decision, Goal, or Strategy?

Prioritize

Were the Most Urgent & Valuable Decisions Made First?

Results

Were the Desired Results Achieved?   In Hindsight, Were the Correct Decisions Made?   Was Execution Greater, Worse, or Same as Desired?

Section Summary & Conclusion

Implementing the strategy is more than informing the staff there is a new course of action, it is a step-by-step process to allow input, educate on how and why the decisions were made, and to communicate relentlessly. Each staff member needs to internalize the direction of the company and the specific tasks for which they are responsible and accountable.

Developing the decision making model will create a more nimble company and extinguish accountability gaps.

1. Outstanding strategy is only achieved with meaningful execution.

2. Obtain inputs and feedback from all levels when formulating strategy.

3. Staff work with the details and have a different perspective than the big picture executives.

4. Buy-in is achieved much quicker and easier when staff ideas are heard and integrated into the plan.

5. Educate and explain, continuously, the new strategy.

6. All members of staff need to be acutely aware of their roles, responsibilities, accountabilities, and how they'll be evaluated. Ambiguity is the enemy, clarity is the goal.

    a. The Strategic Scorecard provides clarity for the company, division, team, and individual goals.

7. Motivating staff is a multistep process, including hiring the right people.

8. Charm your employees, you want the best to stay. Remember, "We want you" is the recruitment pitch.

9. Empower the staff and trust them to make the right decisions.

10. Set clear lines of accountability and responsibility for in-

dividuals, and enable them to make the decisions to effectively manage.

11. Recognize internal decision making bottlenecks and eliminate them.

12. Navigate through internal company politics with precision and with a plan. Do not overlook that politics is a team sport.

13. Avoid the common mistakes and common hurdles. Be mindful of the 'Status Quo Mindset,' 'Inspirational Jump,' 'Risk & Reward Hurdle,' and the 'Deployment Game.'

14. Hire those you believe in.

15. Appoint a Devil's Advocate.

16. Create joint value between the client organization and the supplier by integrating companies through efficiencies and greater operational effectiveness.

17. Seek buy-in on the concept and the details of a plan, do not seek consensus.

18. Recognize the principles of effective decision making and implement these into your strategic framework to create a more nimble and effective company.

Section Five: Marketing Strategy

"Marketing takes a day to learn. Unfortunately it takes a lifetime to master."

PHIL KOLTER, AUTHOR, CONSULTANT, PROFESSOR

"In marketing you must choose between boredom, shouting, and seduction. Which do you want?"

ROY H. WILLIAMS, WIZARD OF ADS

There are an endless number of books and tomes on marketing strategy ranging from the traditional emphasis on FABs (Features, Advantages, and Benefits) to the modernist approach of focusing on the powerful image or storytelling visual with narration downplaying the details (pharmaceutical advertising). Instead of reproducing the all-encompassing surface level highlights into one Section, allow this Section's emphasis on Marketing to focus on the principles to make an effective campaign and to stay relevant once established.

Barriers to Market Adoption

The marketers' goal is not only to bring awareness to a product or service, but also to reach significant levels of adaptation by the consumers or the industry that it serves. Before delving into the principles for an effective campaign, a review of the market barriers to overcome is essential.

The Five A's

The first barrier to adoption is simple Awareness. If the public is not [yet] aware of your product, how or why would they consider purchase?

FIGURE 15: BARRIERS TO MARKET ADOPTION

Barriers to Market Adoption

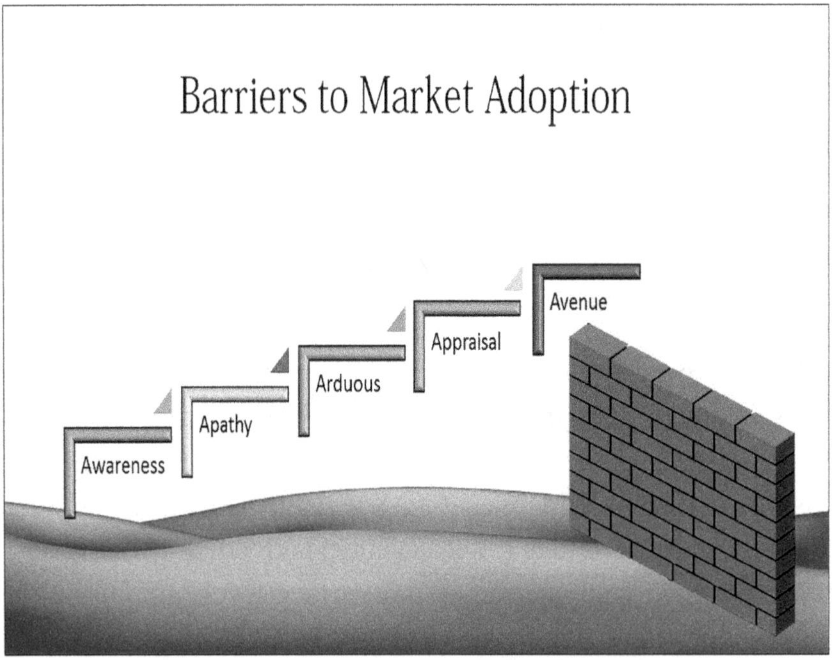

There is an interesting debate on which is worse, if people are unaware of your product, or, if they are aware but not interested? The answer, as almost everything, depends on your perspective. If your organization has spent great treasure on marketing and yet there is little product/service Awareness, the marketing team and/or plan should be scrutinized for its lack of success. Scrap the plan and start anew. Creating a new marketing plan is much simpler than a total reinvention of the business plan and product offering. This leads to the second barrier of Market Adoption, Apathy.

Apathy is when the public is aware of the product, but does not have enough of an interest to become purchasers. A very famous case study of the Apathy barrier is the significant lack of enrollees for the Affordable Care Act, otherwise known as ObamaCare. In history, there are few examples of products or government programs that have received the media and social attention of ObamaCare. But yet, the American public has largely shown dissatisfaction and has not enrolled at rates anywhere near expectations nor projections.

Does your product need a 2,200 page manual explaining how to use it for a consumer, non-technical audience? Are the multiple steps too complex, or arduous? This is the third barrier to market adoption, Arduous tasks to fully gain the value of the product. There are few products that the journey of building or constructing it is the joyous experience that you expect or want, as would be true for Legos, crossword or jigsaw puzzles. Certainly not the basketball hoop in your driveway, or installing the new television or software program. Similar to writing corporate communications, if your middle school aged child at home can't read and understand it, it is most likely overly complicated.

The price offered for a product should to some extent represent its value. This does not mean the highest price offering has the greatest value, nor vice versa, but the price should be an Appraisal of the market. The offering's price should reflect market conditions of supply, demand, and competition. If this appraisal is incorrect and the product is priced too high for the mass market, then this will be a significant barrier to market adoption.

The Avenue represents the distribution network to bring the product to market. Are there limited numbers of outlets for purchase? Or, are the Avenues to reach the consumer difficult to find, work with, or not provide enough attention to the consumer? For example, in a grocery store product location or placement is intensely competitive between suppliers. If the retail outlet will not provide a 'fighting chance' to have your products displayed and sold, it may be time to reevaluate the current distribution network and model for alternatives. In a second example, other Avenues are independent contractors who sell the company's products as part of their portfolio of represented goods but do not properly message and sell the product or service at the desired pace or quantity the manufacturer would prefer.

Individually, each of these steps can sink a product in its voyage towards market adoption. Think of these elements as large steps on a staircase to reach over the barrier for tremendous growth. Each is necessary, requires effort, and none can be skipped over.

Think & Sell in a Narrative

What do stand-up comedians and excellent marketers have in common? Most likely, everyone likes to have a good time after work, but (more importantly) both groups think and share in narratives. The story is how information is passed, not just data, but details are conveyed along with an interesting story that holds your attention. People want to know how a story ends and will want to listen to hear more. A story can be memorable, it can be exciting or interesting, but rarely does a product description match the emotional connection of a narrative.

Within the story are details of a product or an experience that can convey quality, value, or any of the selling factors on which your organization wants to position itself. The story itself is the proof of an experience, and it becomes even more 'truthful' when it is told as a personal narrative. The Four Seasons Hotels aired a television commercial of a man telling a story about his trip to an exotic Four Seasons resort in the South Pacific, complete with details about the food, experience, accommodations, and ending with his unique memento to show how exceptional the visit was. This was not simply an advertisement of the hotel stating how excellent the food and service is, instead there seems to be more credibility as it is told through a narrative by an individual. It is less of a sales pitch, and more of a discovery and sharing of an experience.

An Emotional Journey

The product itself can also be impassioned or emotive, either positively or negatively. When the product is authentically advantageous for people, then the public often become admirers and supporters of the product and/or company behind it. The same can be said of the opposite with a negative connotation, but that of course is a terrible position to be in. These feelings can be expressed and communicated through a powerful story and within a narrative. Each December, as a year-end celebration, Google creates a Zeitgeist[18] video to express "what the world searched for" over the prior twelve months. This is an emotional journey of the sights, sounds, events, triumphs and tribulations of our country and planet. The video begins with the typing of a keyword to perform a search on Google's homepage, and the images

---

18   http://bit.ly/1elrE4A

quickly move from one story to the next as a quick reminder of the

most moving moments; this is the essence capturing the emotion and narrative in a product.

FIGURE 16 GOOGLE'S CORE OFFERING OPENS THE VIDEO, TYPING IN A KEYWORD SEARCH BEFORE THE EMOTIONAL JORNEY BEGINS

These emotional appeals go far beyond the Features, Advantages, & Benefits, and it scraps the boring acronyms. The public wants and needs to experience and feel the product in person, or vicariously through clever advertising. When properly done, the person sitting at home watching on YouTube or on television will feel like they are the ones living the video since they become emotionally attached and a part of the story. The pitch needs to both appear and sound real and authentic. If the plea is for a non-profit organization to benefit suffering people in a far-away land, then the emotional appeal is easy, but it must look and feel credible. The images cannot be simulated or poorly directed, the narration must be excellent, and the details must be exact.

People want to be moved, connected with, entertained, and never sold. Touch their hearts through emotion and you can find a customer.

In business-to-business sales, product demonstrations should also be displayed or conducted in a narrative. Success stories, how the product benefited other customers, etc., all should be told in a story. PowerPoint can be the deathblow to a proposed sale if not used correctly as a tool in telling the story; too often it is infinite boring details displayed on screen. Once the crowd starts to squint to read the endless text on a PowerPoint screen, move through the presentation faster since it is already over.

Some numbers are impressive or difficult to fully comprehend, such as total revenue for booming companies, or the sovereign debt of some nations. Numbers can be amazing but not always captivating. Go one step further to fully communicate the meaning behind the message through imaging.

Imaging is powerful and should be used to the fullest extent in demonstrations, via expressive photos, video, or objects/items to show and tell. It has been stated time and time again because it is true, the image does speak a thousand words. A photo is a brief moment in time, but it speaks of a larger truth such as conflicts, danger, desperation, agony of defeat, or the thrill of victory or triumph. If you understand how a photo can show and produce emotion, you can create equally powerful war or human tragedy images by using images as metaphors in other causes. For example, an image of body bags lining a town square to exhibit the everyday carnage of cancer. A number representing the quantity of deaths from a disease or conflict can be intimidating, but the image will resonate and create the emotional connection. The more personal the story, the better.

Creating the Narrative

To create and develop the narrative, the essential step is selling the dream of what the product can do for you or for society. *'This Water Filter will Save the Planet,' 'BMW is the Ultimate Driving Experience,'* or *'Be the Most Desirable Person in the World.'* The dream doesn't have to be what the product is today, or what it can do for you today, but instead what it inspires to become in the future. Make it emotional, and people will be moved to take action.

What is the product dream? What is envisioned that this product can produce and make right in the world? How does it elevate itself from other similar offerings? Answer these questions and you'll discover your narrative.

FIGURE 17: FRAMEWORK TO FIND THE EMOTION

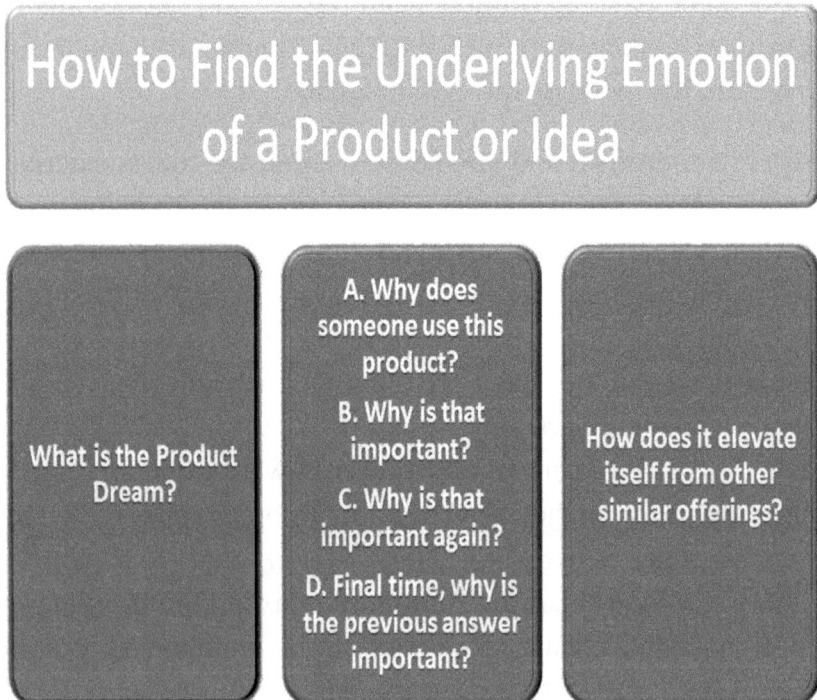

How to Find the Underlying Emotion of a Product or Idea

What is the Product Dream?	A. Why does someone use this product? B. Why is that important? C. Why is that important again? D. Final time, why is the previous answer important?	How does it elevate itself from other similar offerings?

Framing the Conversation

If you don't like what is being said, then change the conversation or, better yet, own the conversation. Successful marketing is not just creating awareness of your product or service, but also framing the message and how the product is viewed or perceived. If the marketers do not define the brand of a product or company, the public will define it for you, for better or worse. Similar to a political candidate, if they do not state what they believe in or what they represent, their opposition can easily make allegations ranging from the inaccurate to the devious; it will certainly not be to the candidate's benefit. Fill the information vacuum with the conversation you want the public to have about your product or service, not what someone else says about it.

Frame the conversation on the significant points of what the product or service generates in real benefits. Excellent charities do not raise money for the sake of having an endowment, instead it is to 'educate future generations,' or to 'feed starving families on Thanksgiving.' Products should also be represented in the benefits they provide; instead of describing office furniture construction as double bolted with triple ply fabric, frame it as 'rarely replaced, lasts for at least a generation.' Skip the technical specifications of a consumer electrics in the tag line, it is not how many megabytes or gigabytes, but instead how many movies and photos the device can hold.

To evaluate the quality of the message, ask yourself if this information will help the potential customer decide between products, and drive demand towards your own.

All Publicity is Good Publicity?

A frequent discussion is whether there is such thing as bad publicity. One point of view is that all publicity is good publicity, and the only problem is having none. Going one step further, publicity is excellent if your product is essential to the story, and good if only your company name is part of the story. On the other hand, if the company and the products are only an afterthought to the story then there is no great positive or negative influence since the unimportant details will be forgotten quickly.

When the product stays in the publics' mind it can produce greater awareness and better sales. If the product is not integral to the story, then there is no real benefit. A critically acclaimed advertisement (named Top 10 of 2013 by Adweek[19]) created by British soft drink company Robinsons received publicity and millions of YouTube views because of its touching and emotional story about fathers and sons[20]. Although millions viewed the advertisement in a positive light, it is not obvious who created the advertisement since the product is irrelevant to the story line. You may need to watch twice to really notice this is a soft drink company and not a Hallmark card. A beautifully created advertisement, excellent buzz surrounding the video, but no bottom line increase of sales due to lack of buzz or attention on Robinsons or their product.

19   bit.ly/WhtPPv
20   bit.ly/1l3qIzN

Robinsons 'Pals'

FIGURE 18 TOUCHING, EMOTIVE, BUT WHERE IS THE DRINK?

Generating publicity and buzz to increase sales is not limited to paid advertising, it can also arise from news events, either positive or negative. Microsoft has been implicated via classified document releases in aiding the National Security Agency (NSA) by allowing access to their customer data in 2013. Only mentioned in the fine details are which products and services Microsoft is alleged to have used to assist the NSA. In this case, the user data that has (possibly) been accessed is held in their Cloud Services, but instead of bringing clear attention to the Cloud Services product on offer, the entire company endures a trust and credibility crisis. There has been no great benefit to the company since the product itself, the Cloud Services, has not received direct attention and greater mass media interest to generate new sales opportunities. It is not important to mention this detail in retelling the story, so hence no publicity surrounding it.

Certainly the advice is not to become embroiled in a scandal or in an otherwise negative fashion, but instead use this principle in a positive constructive way in creating effective advertising. The idea is to create a buzz, and to have your product be essential to the surrounding talk and sharing of your story. If the company, and ideally the product, is not essential to the story then that detail will be left out as it is retold and shared several times over.

Descriptives & Taglines

For the public to understand and remember your product or service, the message behind it needs to be succinct and descriptive. A growing school of thought considers taglines to be a relic of marketing past and the more modern equation is to concentrate on mobile, social media, and highly targeted brand messaging to the particular audience they wish to engage. The concept is there is no longer a one size fits all tagline to reach every market and demographic; the new 'flexible' branding concept presents a different identity to each audience. For instance, Best Buy advertises their Geek Squad service to small business whereas younger customers are targeted through mobile offerings and advertising. Best Buy does not have a consistent identity nor tagline across all platforms.

Companies have also moved away from taglines for they often do not represent the full personality of a brand that exhibits their values and personalities. Instead, the tagline is pithy, by definition, and can only provide a glimpse into the entire branding message. However, the tagline is still an excellent method to communicate a simple and direct message, whether it is a new company or an attempt to refocus or redefine an existing brand. It should be noted, unless the company uses the tagline often, it is not worth using at all. Repetition and consistency are necessary for successful tagline implementation.

Descriptives slightly differ from taglines as they describe the product or service using similes, metaphors, or short statements, whereas the tagline is generally more of a statement. The descriptives can be used interchangeably between taglines, or used in addition to a tagline. Arguably, in some cases they are the same thing.

There are a few suggestions, not rules, to formulate your messaging for either a tagline or a descriptive. First, think in 3s.

Ready. Set. Golf. by Volkswagen for the VW Golf

The Few. The Proud. The Marines by the United States Marine Corps

The second suggestion is to keep it pithy. Below are two well-known taglines:

We Try Harder by Avis

Never Leave Home Without It by American Express

The descriptors are often metaphors to draw an easy connection between the value the product offers and the real benefit that is easily understood and remembered. The metaphor can bring abstract ideas to life quickly, and without tremendous explanation via statements or through images or video. Of course it does not need to be literal, or truthful when presented in an exaggerated manner such that the parody is obvious.

Your Daily Ray of Sunshine by Tropicana, makers of orange juice

It's What Comfort Food Tastes Like by Werther's, the candy company's bid to make consumers feel good about eating their candy.

Think Outside the Bun by Taco Bell

Similes use the same principles, but are comparisons:

The service on Virgin Airlines was like dinner at Buckingham Palace by Virgin Airlines

Like a Rock by Chevy

Party Like a Rockstar by Rockstar Energy Drink

To construct a simile or metaphor for your own marketing, start with the most basic idea and the key concept for the product. What solution or benefit does it provide? Next, complete this sentence:

"Or brand/service/product is like or similar to . . ."

"The consumer benefits from this brand/service/product is like or similar to . . ."

Next, remove the 'like or similar to' and the metaphor can be formed.

A few tips when creating the simile or metaphor, they should be unique and not related to any other products or services existing narrative. Second, allow the claims to be genuine unless they are made in gest to the extremes, but that should also be obvious to all, not just those internal to the company.

Finally, caveat emptor to those who create scare tactic messaging. In politics fear is exceptionally effective for it drives citizens to the polls to vote against the candidate they dread, accurately or not. For consumers, the opposite is true. If toothpaste companies create negative pitches against another then toothpaste sales in general will decrease. If the pitch is created poorly as a scare tactic as to why someone should use your product, there are generally unintended consequences and such pitches rarely work. The safest route is to remain positive for your own product, against the competitors, and avoid all negativity.

Generating Word of Mouth Buzz

Almost everyone socializes at work, via activities at night or on the weekend, online, or on the phone. All of these times are opportunities to discuss good experiences and less than desirable experiences. How often have you mentioned a favorite restaurant, café, or a movie you couldn't wait to go see? Young parents discuss baby products, soccer teams discuss which cleats are the best on the pitch, and businessmen chat about vendors and deliverables. Yes, it sounds stereotyped, but it is true.

McKinsey & Company research suggests word of mouth is the primary factor in-between 20 to 50 percent of all purchasing decisions. This influence is most pronounced in expensive purchases, coupled with consumer research, collecting of opinions, and a longer sales cycle.

If the person sharing an opinion is a highly credible and trustworthy authority, then without surprise their recommendation may carry significant weight in decision making. An interesting side note, positive opinions are shared more often than negative opinions.

To generate word of mouth about your product or service, obliviously people need to be made aware of it and may also have experienced it. Wherever possible due to the product type, offer a free and promotional trial. Allow the process to be easy and user friendly without obstructions to find and experience the product without the need of training or guidance. The no obligation trial should only cost the user's time, and within this period the product needs to prove its value and benefits.

The simpler the process, the higher the probability of user interaction and spreading positive word of mouth.

Not every product will be revolutionary or society changing, but products can escape the mold of ordinary by surpassing expectations and/or breaking an apparent or recognized pattern. When products are above and beyond the industry norm, they generate buzz and hence word of mouth.

In 2005, Woodford Reserve, the official Bourbon of the Kentucky Derby unveiled the $1,000 Mint Julep Cup to be purchased and celebrated at the annual 'Run for the Roses' with proceeds benefitting the Old Friends Retirement Center, which supports retired thoroughbred horses. The cups feature an elaborate gold plated medallion complete with a gold sipping straw and was made available only in limited quantities of less than one hundred. The word of mouth buzz was scintillating and the cups sold out quickly with high demand for more. If the Mint Julep Cup was $15, $100 or $200 would it have similar buzz or exposure? Not likely. The $1,000 cup broke the common perception of what a cup or drink should cost and stood above the ordinary. Break the mold, emphasize what is extraordinary, provide some exclusivity, and word of mouth will follow.

FIGURE 19: WOODFORD RESERVE 'RUN FOR THE ROSES' MINT JULEP CUP

Staying Top of Mind

There is a science for products to be remembered or thought

about during the day; it is not just clever advertising that is funny, emotional, or touching in some method. The concept is for everyday life and occurrences to remind you of the product. Jonah Berger in his book CONTAGIOUS refers to this concept as 'Triggers,' environmental reminders for related concepts and ideas.

An environmental trigger may be background music that is associated with a product due to previous advertising campaigns or an association of similarity (Asian music towards Asian food), a specific color associated with an organization or cause, or scents reminiscent of a type of food such as breads or meats, or a specific smell of a type of cheese. When your mind recognizes the scent, music or color, either subconsciously or consciously, you'll be reminded of the product or cause. Since the 2008 National Football League (NFL) season, each October has been designated by the league as Breast Cancer Awareness month for community outreach. The field, players' uniforms, and referee uniforms have various pink accents as the representative color to develop awareness, as do other breast cancer awareness campaigns. Due to the consistent color identity and connection, in theory, when people see pink it should remind them of breast cancer and hopefully spark action to be tested for the disease or to donate funds for research.

An effective stimulus would be frequent in everyday life such as driving a car, drinking coffee, or checking email. What are the many frequent and daily actions of the target audience that can be manipulated to build a mental bridge to connect and remind consumers of your product or service? A Virginia based software firm created a linkage between their system protection services and their core customers, the IT department, who frequently communicate through internal instant messaging. Through repetition and clever marketing, each time the IT staff member opens their instant message program, they are reminded of this firm.

When you see the color pink, do you think of Victoria's Secret? Breast Cancer? Or wide receiver gloves worn by NFL players? All three are appropriate, and two of the three are related. How about the color gold? Are you reminded of money, Donald Trump's buildings in New York City, and/or jewelry? Many colors have associations with tangible products, movements, or feelings. Red is love and Valentine's Day. Do you think of Ferrari when you see red? Perhaps not, only a small fraction would.

FIGURE 20: KEYS FOR AN EFFECTIVE TRIGGER

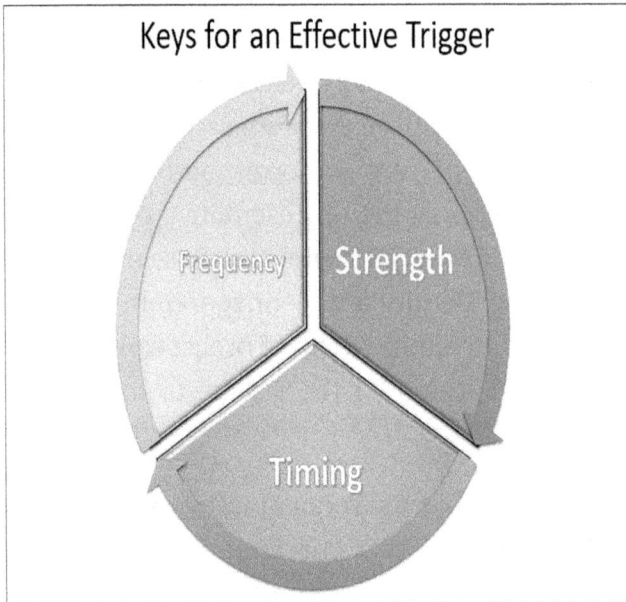

Keys for an Effective Trigger

The ubiquitousness of some colors in correlation to brands, identities, or products deny the power of the color to be a trigger. The less often used the color is in representing other movements or products the better or easier it will be to transform that color into your own identity and brand. For best results, use an original and distinctive environmental factor (a factor seen in everyday life and in your daily surroundings) that is unused by other firms or organizations. This is a measurement of the strength of the trigger, how well the color, music, or action ties in to your message.

The third category in creating an effective trigger is accurate timing between the trigger and the call to action, such as a purchase or similar determination. If the targeted daily environmental trigger is taking a shower, there are not many call to actions during this active time, no purchases (at least very unlikely) are being made in the shower. Any action will be delayed by several minutes which could be enough time for the trigger or action to be forgotten. Albeit, the person is going to make decisions in the shower about soap and/or shampoo, and hence this can be decided in the shower. However, purchasing soap or shampoo does not occur in the shower, and the purchase action would have to be delayed and the trigger is lost.

Monkey See, Monkey Do

People are drawn to the actions, thoughts, and fashions of other people and often imitate. Fashion designers plaster their name across t-shirts, purses, and other garb not just as a fashion statement or pure publicity, but also to bring social acceptance to their name and brand. If a beautiful women wears an outfit with designer XYZ sprawled across the front, then credibility is carried to the brand for all (or at least many) who see this display.

Very often people follow the crowd and imitate what they see others using or doing. Have you been to the movie theatre and seen a long line for a particular screen and wondered what film you may be missing? How often do you dine at an empty restaurant during peak hours instead of the crowded eatery across the street? If this does not describe you, then perhaps you are the distinct minority and generally considered an outlier.

Jonah Berger points out that laugh tracks are added into television shows so the viewing audience at home is more comfortable, aware of when to laugh, and because laughing is CONTAGIOUS.

To make use of the 'follow the crowd' concept for marketing purposes, follow two rules to reach success. First, the product itself should be accessible for everyone to see the purchaser consuming or making use of the product. Second, target key influencers who will help sway and adjust the market towards your product.

Highly Visible
• Product is consumed for all to see & imitate

Key Influencers
• Disproportionate sway over market

FIGURE 21: THE PRODUCT SHOULD BE SEEN, SO IT CAN BE IMITATED

In the earlier example of a beautiful women displaying a designer's name and brand, she, in theory, is able to influence others because of her beauty and hence credibility in fashion. Is it fair or right? Absolutely not, but it is reality. The first point of this example is that the brand label was highly visible so all can see, read, and know what the brand is. The second point, if not already clear, is that she has disproportionate influence because of her beauty. On a larger scale, we see this same type of influence for products from paid and unpaid celebrities in commercials or being photographed walking down the street. The product needs to be shown clearly so people can imitate it. Apple chose white head phones for the introduction of the iPod to separate from the competition and to show market ubiquitousness. Once the white headphones were seen all over the town, it appears as through 'everyone' has one, and you must have one too.

Also in the world of Apple, the Macintosh logo illuminates and faces outward when the laptop is being operated. Walk into a Manhattan coffee café on a Sunday afternoon and try not to be blinded by intense logo luminosities. The room, or the public, can see which laptop brand you own and operate and this brings credibility to the product and the company – 'if everyone uses this brand, then so must I.' These products advertise themselves as the consumers use them for their intended purpose.

In industries there are thought leaders who hold disproportionate influence within their markets. Goldman Sachs is widely considered a thought leader in corporate finance, and the actions of super-majors ExxonMobil and Shell are followed closely in the Oil and Gas Industry. Their decisions on which areas to explore, products and technologies to purchase and deploy, and organizational behavior are often imitated by smaller competing firms. They serve as thought leaders and hold disproportionate influence on this industry.

In both national politics and/or the politics within a company, there are personalities and power wielders that can influence a policy or a product decision far beyond the abilities of the average person within these organizations. If you're able to influence the correct company or person, they will be able to disproportionately alter the market in your favor.

Section Summary & Conclusion

Marketing is more than bringing awareness to a product, it must be a well-conceived strategy to create a connection with the consumer and to reach market adaptation. This connection can be emotional, it could be created from significant word of mouth buzz, or the brand/product has been observed publicly so often there is a desire to fit in with the crowd. These characteristics can all be created or manufactured and are not the result of luck.

Below are the fundamental concepts and actionable items presented in this Section:

1. Significant sales growth is achieved when there is consumer adoptation in the market or industry, not just awareness.

2. Overcome the common market barriers to adoption (Five A's).

3. Tell the product story in a narrative, not just highlighting or screaming the details.

4. Be emotional and connect with the audience. Entertain with a purpose.

5. Images and video are extremely powerful, and far more connecting than words on a page or a screen.

6. Find the underlying emotion of the product or idea by discovering why the product matters. What does it really do, go deeper to discover the meaning behind it.

7. Define the brand the way you want it to be, not as the public or others will define it for you.

8. When creating publicity (events, emotive advertising), be

sure your name, product, or brand is essential to retelling the story to become the story, not an irrelevant detail.

9. Taglines are effective at concisely delivering the message and defining the brand.

10. Use similes, metaphors, think in threes.

11. Word of mouth is an extremely powerful tool in developing sales.

12. Be extraordinary, unexpected, or outside of the normal boundaries to generate exposure and word of mouth buzz.

13. Linking an everyday item through repetition to your product can create a reminder to think about purchasing, using, and consuming a product.

    a. Can work with objects, activities, colors, etc.

14. Not all reminders or Triggers are equally effective.

15. Highly visible products (wearing a brand's clothes, drinking from a brand's mug, driving a certain model car) bring not only credibility to brands, but also a desire to fit in with everyone else. They create 'must haves.'

Section Six: Sales Strategy Execution

A really great talent finds its happiness in execution.

JOHANN WOLFGANG VON GOETHE, STATESMAN, WRITER

*However beautiful the strategy, you should
occasionally look at the results*

SIR WINSTON CHURCHILL, PRIME MINISTER, UNITED KINGDOM

Revenue is the lifeblood of any organization, it touches and breathes life into every corner. Revenue lands in many forms, ranging from product sales direct to the end user, through distributors, as charitable donations, and as seed or investment funds for startups or growth. In every case, revenue is the result of a strategy (usually executed by the sales team) to obtain the sale by convincing someone to part with their money.

The sales team is a vital arm of any organization, for its work cannot be outsourced, and you cannot operate without them. Also, no matter how useful or important your product, with rare exceptions, it won't sell without a sales effort. Hence, there is a special focus on how to manage this team as part of your corporate strategy.

This section will explain the creation of the most efficient and successful sales strategy execution program for your organization. This can be applied to non-profits, for-profits large and small, and every type of industry.

New Organizational Strategy, New Processes

The sales team is the tip of the spear, the deal makers, the revenue producers, and often the face of the company to potential and existing clients. There are numerous tomes on the science of sales by matching personalities, clever manipulative statements in response to customer actions, and basic cold call scripts. Instead of rehashing the common points, this section will focus on the management processes to ensure both a successful improvement strategy, and the execution of the corporate strategy.

How to develop a sales improvement strategy? Process and planning. The process begins with an evaluation of the current environment including sales levels, wins/losses, sales skills, and leadership skills of the managerial team supporting the sales staff. Once the evaluation is complete, the areas in need of improvement will be apparent and it will be possible to then design and build the skill enhancement process for the team including managerial staff.

The next step in the process is to carry out the training program, to be followed by tracking the progress and success rate of each member. Review for improvement. And repeat.

FIGURE 22: SALES IMPROVEMENT STRATEGY PROCESS

Sales Improvement Strategy Process

Evaluation Phase
Create Improvement Process
Implementation & Training
Track Progress
Repeat

Evaluation Phase

The evaluation process is not limited to testing sales skills and quantitative assessment of transactions, opportunities, and conversion to sales for each member of the team. This is the time to evaluate the buy-in of the company's culture and values, and the new or existing strategy, and to determine if the organization can offer what each staff member expects or wants from the professional relationship. There are several questions to ask during the evaluation, including:

1. Does each staff member buy-in on their strategy execution scorecard containing the company, division, team, and individual goals? (see Section Four)

2. Is the culture of the sales team consistent, and is it consistent with the rest of the company?

3. Is the accountability model understood, agreed upon, and
    is there an effective deterrent for non-performance?

To evaluate whether the sales division and members holds the
same values of the company and/or the other members of the sales
team or division, these values must already be defined. The Core
Ideology and Strategic Principle have been addressed in Section
One, but go deeper to determine which are the most important
values to hold, and which to avoid. Organizations have a tremendous range in values including the number of hours to work, how
to dress, communication norms, and the level of expected work /
life balance sacrifices to make. The sales division may approach
this entirely different than the accounting staff, and junior and
senior sales people could have tremendously varying definitions
as well.

Communicate these values with consistency, and be sure they are
clear during job interviews so you only hire the best fit for the
company.

The second area of the evaluation phase are the quantitative mea-
surements. What are the norms in your industry and how does
each member of the sales team compare with closing ratios, number of pipeline and sales funnel opportunities? If these metrics do
not exist, it is time to create the infrastructure to track the performance. There will be pushback from more senior staff who will
most likely share this thought, "I've always done it this way, now
leave me alone." The sales and opportunity metrics must exist in
order to create an effective accountability model and to track performance. Even though the senior staff may be the top 20% in the
80/20 rule, there is always room for improvement and no one will
know to what extent without the proper oversight. Everyone has
oversight, from the entry level to the CEO.

Selling is a skill to be mastered, much like cooking or playing
basketball. Some people have an easier time than others due to
personality and natural ability, but the greatest athletes in the

world trained for over 10,000 hours before becoming profession-als. How long do sales people train for? There are skills that must be learned, and not just acquired through experience (you may be experienced in all of the wrong habits). This is the time to ad-minister examinations (these can be easily found on the internet with basic searching, or contact the author of this book) to the sales staff. The exercise is not to rank or to reveal a final score out of 100 that determines who is great and who is dreadful. Instead, the purpose of the self-examination is to identify the specific skill areas that range from poor to great so they can be improved as needed. For example, if fictional salesperson Carlos scores poor-ly on organizational abilities, then his upcoming training will be focused on this particular area and future follow up will concen-trate yet again until his abilities are great, and not just average.

The evaluation will also discover each members sales process, whether that is intuitive, or structured and deliberate. Are they following preconceived and clear steps, or is it make it up as you go along? Is there consistency across all members of the team? Hopefully, it is consistency in a positive manner, and not everyone being consistently incorrect.

Leadership ability and quality are essential to building a solid and effective team; this too must be evaluated to discover the areas in need of improvement (examinations can also be found on the in-ternet with basic searching, or contact the author). Have multiple members of the leadership team take the evaluation about them-selves, and also evaluate each other. For more honest and accu-rate evaluations, allow for confidential peer scoring by a third party to gather the information and collate the per section scores for each member of the leadership. Having your own skills evalu-ated by peers is a valuable window into how others perceive your strengths and weaknesses and an opportunity to improve. You will not be an effective leader if those around you do not believe you have all of the skills.

The sales team should also be given the opportunity to confidentially evaluate their sales management; this is a learning and improvement process. If you are unaware of a problem, then you aren't going to fix it.

Designing the Improvement Process

The Improvement Process is the strategy to improve the sales teams' performance, consistency, and overall effectiveness. The first step was to determine the baseline from which the skills and process would be built; this second step is the designing and building of the strategy using the information learned from the evaluation on what changes are needed. This is the 'how.'

Building Best Practices

Carlos, the fictional salesperson who became aware of his lack of organizational skills after the self-evaluation, is ready for improvement in this area and in multiple other steps in the selling process such as competitive intelligence and properly communicating the company's message/value to prospective clients. How to do so? During an all hands on deck sales meeting, the sales team with the aid of management will build best practices on all steps in their sales cycle and process in a group effort. Before gathering the staff, research articles that describe success stories and winning processes for your specific industry and/or products.

Have each member of the sales team define the company's message and value either aloud or on paper, then compile the concepts onto a single white board or the like. Re-review the value curves created (from Section Three) to study how your product or service differs from the competition and the unique value that you're selling. Brainstorm and have discussions to determine the best method to present this information (elevator pitch, presentation formula) and course of action.

This type of procedure is to be repeated for the various sections of the sales process and cycle, including prospecting, selling skills, organization, messaging, and/or obtaining competitive intelligence. The concept is to formulate conclusions and decisions using practitioner inputs of what has previously worked well, and what was less than ideal. Since the sales staff is aiding and contributing to this process, the buy-in will be much greater than if the processes were purely dictated to them.

Collaborating in a group environment enhances the 'team' concept that is often attempted in sales organizations, but not realized since the majority of their work is highly individual. In an 'every person for themselves' environment it is rare that information and learning is passed along. By creating a team atmosphere, mistakes and success stories can be shared to spare others the same pitfalls and to streamline to find the most successful process for greater success. When one learns, everyone learns.

When best practices are established, the team will be able to offer a consistent message to all clients and, in particular, by multiple members of the sales team to the same client during larger sales opportunities. If different messages are presented to the same client, your sales team will appear to be unprofessional, liars, and/or fools. This will be reflected in missed sales opportunities.

The best practices also serve as a new goal for planning future training and coaching. The original baseline conceived through self-evaluation represented the current skills of the team. However, a definition of success is necessary to compare the results against. For example, if Carlos believes his messaging is excellent and scored himself a five out of five on the evaluation, what should his score be now that he learned his messaging did not meet the newly established goals and was incorrect and needs improvement? The best practices will serve as the standard for future evaluation and for the coaches to use as a playbook.

Implementing the Sales Strategy

The sales strategy implementation step is a confluence of corporate strategy, divisional strategy, team, personal, and best practices into one. The Strategic Scorecard tool will assist in communicating both the macro and micro strategy to the sales team, but now the best practices will also need to be integrated. Do not assume your sales staff is motivated and ready to use the best practices that were formulated once they are back in the field or at work. Start by asking for commitments and discover any hesitancies that may inhibit execution.

There are several methods to motivate staff beyond financial incentives of commission and bonuses. Recognizing that management leads people and only manages processes is the first step towards friendly relations with the sales staff. People are highly motivated, but often motivated by very different things. Some employees are motivated to become famous as musicians, and not to sell photocopiers. Other employees want to become CEOs and are looking beyond their sales results for the next two quarters and thinking about how to move up into a higher role. Your task is to create the environment where people can motivate themselves to sell your product.

FIGURE 23: METHODS TO MOTIVATE STAFF

Motivational Tools

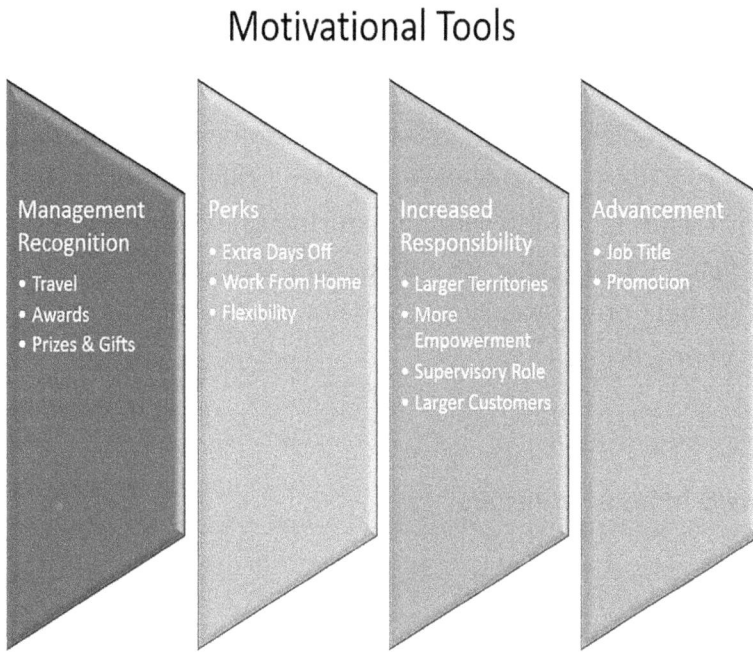

Management Recognition	Perks	Increased Responsibility	Advancement
• Travel • Awards • Prizes & Gifts	• Extra Days Off • Work From Home • Flexibility	• Larger Territories • More Empowerment • Supervisory Role • Larger Customers	• Job Title • Promotion

Creating clearly defined and achievable goals is an important element of achieving buy-in, and for the implementation process. For sales staff, this is exceptionally important to the compensation model and is the raison d'etre of why many are in the sales field. In the Oil & Gas Industry, there is a service company specializing in safety equipment that redefined their compensation model to a formula of all or nothing (the first commission payout only occurs when the quota is reached) coupled with an exceptionally high quota. Many of the salespeople who did not leave the firm found it was not 'worth their effort' to attempt new sales. These salespeople had little or no confidence a commission would be earned because they believed they could not reach the astronomically high quota where initial quota payouts would occur. To refer to this company's employees as unmotivated is a tremendous understatement.

Developing a congenial and team atmosphere builds confidence and motivation. Football teams, the Armed Forces, and trapeze artists work together as a team and the camaraderie is a motivating factor to perform well not just for yourself, but for the others surrounding you.

Implementation also includes continual training to remind staff of the best practices and to always improve skills. Training can be in many forms, including seminars during sales meetings, phone conferences, one-on-one meetings, and partnering with other staff members on customer visits to see and hear different techniques in practice.

Tracking & Measuring Results

Develop a performance plan for all sales people to set clear expectations and openly share how the numbers were derived, the rewards for doing well, and the consequences of not reaching the goals. Favor the carrot over the stick. Creating and explaining the expectations will provide structure and transparency for the management and staff. Re-visit progress with each staff member either monthly or quarterly to increase the odds of success and to correct any incorrect actions or inactions early.

The tracking system, most likely a CRM program, must measure the wins, losses, opportunities created, sales funnel, conversion percentages, etc. With a new corporate strategy, and increased internal training for the sales staff, there should be an increase of revenue and noticeable statistical differences for year-on-year performance.

Beyond tracking sales numbers and sales cycle statistics, it is crucial to re-evaluate your sales staff selling and process abilities on roughly a quarterly or bi-annual basis to track performance. If improvement is not consistently being made, then you'll be aware of specific areas on which to focus additional training and resources to generate more productivity and, ultimately, revenue.

If there are technical aspects to the sale, such as equipment, machinery, electronics, be sure to invest in making the sales team fluent in the specifications or the key technical information that is necessary to the customer, and to the sale. If possible, have the technical staff at your company sit with the sales staff and explain the product and its unique features. Create an exam for the sales staff to test their knowledge of the relevant technical specifications. No more than fifteen or twenty questions are necessary to determine who knows their product, and who does not. It may be eye opening to find a lack of knowledge, and this may be the key inhibitor for continued sales growth.

Obtaining Leverage

How to win more deals and increase sales? Obtain leverage, and leverage equals power. Leverage is recognizing the need of the other party and having what they want, whether that is information, product, or a service. In movies and television shows we often see leverage as a form of blackmail or some other devious method. Just to be clear, that is not the advice here, but it serves as an example to relate to the power of removing or preventing pain to a potential client by providing a needed solution.

There are many forms of leverage that may not be apparent and some may result from pure luck.

Here is a unique example in a non-complementary business that may relate to a situation for your own business. Recently in the National Basketball Association (NBA) a Point Guard of average ability and productivity signed a massively lucrative contract well above the pay rate for his accomplishments. He wasn't extremely popular, didn't sell many jerseys, fans were not eager to watch him in person or on television as they would a representational athlete like Jeremy Lin (significant following among Asian-Americans and throughout Asia). Why was he able to negotiate such a substantial contract? Leverage. The new team needed a Point Guard and there were very few of average abilities or better to choose from. The other Point Guards in the NBA were already under contract. Essentially, it was a sellers' market and pure luck for him that his previous contract terminated at that time.

Create a sellers' market by differentiating your product enough, but yet still appealing to a mass market as discussed in Section Three, through realigning your value curve. When there are few choices and a need exists, leverage is borne.

Also, integrating your company into the clients will make it difficult and sometimes costly to switch to a new vendor. This may include shared R&D, shared facilities, or project implementation. The more you are integrated, the simpler it will be to win new business across additional platforms or divisions either locally, or in other regions. Building excellent rapport and goodwill internally is the key for future business wins from people within the company whom you've never met, but who will still need your services.

Leverage is like poker, don't always show your hand. Never let the purchaser or client know how much you need their business. Desperation can be seen and felt a mile away and many will take advantage of the situation through a one sided contract and terms. As a service provider, you need to either be able to, or provide the impression that you'll be able to walk away and are not in need of their business. Show strength and be confident of the value of your offering.

Position yourself and stay on the offensive by offering new R&D and diversification of the supply chain to ensure the client company cannot circumvent you and go directly to your own suppliers, and/or bring your operations in-house, subsequently replacing your firm in either case. Continue to adjust the value and service and not be flanked by your own client. This could be especially true if you're a distributor and the client company could purchase directly from the manufacturer. First, your manufacturer must not supplant your business and deal directly with the end client. If they would, you need to find a new supplier. Secondly, you'll need to offer products and a service that cannot be obtained by any other manufacturers that would sell direct to the end user.

For example, the wholesale lighting industry is quite diversified with numerous factories that build LEDs throughout Asia. Large companies could contract directly with the manufacturer in China and circumvent distributors altogether. To play defense, this distributor will need to find more and different products to build a consortium of offerings that cannot be easily replicated, and increase the level of service to efficiently move and deliver the final end products, in addition to having more leeway on product quantities either large or small. In person consultative service is also very helpful to help the client select the products, just be careful they don't use the selected specifications to have this product made someplace else. Leverage all of your other offerings and remain relevant, position your service to be about quality, service, and the various technologies you have on offer. Don't let it rest squarely on price.

Holding Intellectual Property is excellent leverage, it is the power of being the only one on the block with the new toy. The only difficulty is in creating a unique and powerful tool, device, or process that is in heavy demand and warrants significant expenditures.

The final element of leverage is information. This information could include the costs associated with the project, or budget allocated for your product or service. Similar to purchasing an automobile from a dealership, if you're aware of the invoice price (the sale amount the dealer purchased from the manufacturer) you can begin your negotiations from this starting point. If you're interviewing for a new job and you discover this position has been allocated a budget of $100,000 salary per year, would you request $85,000 in salary?

Information is also relevant if your organization is aware of inside information about the processes and other confidential information about the client. Perhaps this information was learned from a relationship of trust and prior integration, but most often keeping this information tight knit and allowing fewer people and firms to know about it would be a priority for the client, resulting in increased leverage for the supplier in future negotiations.

Sales Leadership

What is the definition or the purpose of sales leadership? Some may say "to lead," or to hold the staff accountable to their duties and responsibilities. Although those are aspects for the role of sales leader, it misses the purpose and the underlying core. The objective of sales leadership is to increase productivity and revenue beyond the levels that would be achieved without their involvement. Additionally, the sales leadership should assist the staff in getting deeper, higher, and wider in accounts to further integrate the companies and create additional selling opportunities, or to assist in closing the initial sale.

Many organizations have an 80/20 rule whether that refers to a non-profit's fundraising, or a high-tech manufacturer's sales efforts. The 80/20 rule, also known as the Pareto Principle, states that roughly 80% of the outcome is generated from 20% of the activity. In other words, 20% of your accounts will represent 80% of the revenue. Or the top 20% of your sales force, will generate 80% of total sales. If for whatever reason it has not already been analyzed, identify and acknowledge these accounts to further integrate your companies immediately.

These accounts essentially 'keep the lights on' and should be awarded the proper amount of respect and attention. When was the last time senior management visited these accounts? How often does the VP of sales, or VP of Fundraising visit with these top purchasers and donors? How about the 'C' level? When appropriate, consider setting multiple meetings per year (perhaps on a quarterly basis), to go beyond alleviating any potential problems or issues, but instead to make the relationship more personal and deeper. Show you care as if the life of the business depends on it, because it does. Don't take the top 20% for granted, instead, shower them with the goodwill that is necessary to keep the company not only prosperous, but alive.

For maximum effectiveness, the leadership should recognize its role as 'leader' and not the chief go-getter or doer. Leadership needs to efficiently delegate, be proactive and focused on long-term results, and internally sell the vision and strategy of the company, division, and team. Within this role, they also need to be balanced between an objective number cruncher, a coach, and an enforcer of expectations – a disciplinarian.

A proactive leader is highly focused on actions, and not just discussing visions and concepts. This role involves discussing the growth plans for each salesperson, focusing on the most important accounts, and strategizing how to achieve significant growth. To be proactive is to inquire and evaluate all areas and staff you are responsible for, and not waiting until there is a problem to take action and be involved. Regular strategy sessions with staff will enable problems to be caught before they mushroom into a larger situation. Identify what has happened, what is planned, and the next steps to reach the selling goals.

A successful executive asks the right questions to their staff to examine all avenues and gain perspective, sometimes open ended, other times pointed. Asking the sales staff many questions such as, "what happens next?," "have you considered. . . ," and "what other methods can we use?" will inspire staff to creative and unique thinking, and develop the strategy deeper to think multiple steps ahead. The goal is to have staff answer their own questions once they recognize and solve the problem in a different point of view. Use the time with staff to strategize, and allow them to create their own ideas to test and implement.

Section Summary & Conclusion

Sales teams rarely outperform the strategy and the skills of their leadership, so it is the responsibility of the management and senior management to create the best possible tactics, the supporting training, and the tools for implementation. Remember, the basic definition of a sales manager is to "allow the team to perform better than if they were left alone." Provide the training, provide the structure, and provide the strategic direction of the company.

Below are the fundamental concepts and actionable items presented in this Section:

1. Revenue is a key driver of company failure and success, consequently the sales team and sales strategy requires special attention.

2. Management processes must be planned and deliberate; follow a regimented game plan of:

    a. Evaluation

    b. Improvement Process

    c. Training & Implementation

    d. Tracking Progress

    e. Repeat

3. Determine the skills and the current quantifiable sales metrics to be used as a baseline.

4. Create the best practices.

5. Discover how the members of your sales team are motivated, and create the environment so they can motivate themselves to sell more.

6. Track results and consistently monitor performance and evaluate skills.

7. Create a consequence model of not achieving the sales goals, and communicate clearly the evaluation criteria and penalties.

8. Leverage can be created and will increase the ability to sell for larger profits.

9. Be a pro-active sales leader not by micromanaging, but by asking questions and pushing staff to think multiple steps ahead.

10. Recognize the 80/20 accounts, and integrate as much as possible.

Section Seven: Expanding Internationally

"If things seem under control, you're just not going fast enough."
MARIO ANDRETTI, RACING DRIVER

"I am always doing that which I cannot do, in order that I may learn how to do it."
PABLO PICASSO, ARTIST

People who don't travel cannot have a global view, all they see is what's in front of them. Those people cannot accept new things because all they know is where they live.
MARTIN YAN, CHEF

4.4%. This is the percentage of the world's population who lives in America. When the market focus is solely the United States, then you are ignoring over 95% of the world. International expansion can elevate a good company to greatness by multiplying its revenues via expansion to more markets and by reaching more people and companies than ever before.

Most often, companies who have the potential to expand internationally do not do so for one or more of these three reasons: (1)

they do not know how, (2) they do not even consider it, and/or (3), potential risk.

This chapter will detail how to successfully expand internationally and the common pitfalls to avoid. First, a note on risk. The business risks associated with market expansion will be detailed in this section. However, there are big picture or strategic risks to consider that rise above the details and should be addressed. If the company or organization does not expand overseas, what is the risk in comparison to the competition? What are the risks of non-expansion?

With international expansion, there is an opportunity to create partners who will not compete in your core domestic market but who can jointly share research and development costs to enhance your competitive advantage. The question should be asked, when will your competition expand overseas and will you be able to compete if they do?

Floods, droughts, currency fluctuation, labor strikes, are all localized events and elements of risk when expanding internationally, but they are also elements of risk **domestically**. If your firm is localized to one region or country, these events have the potential to substantially affect your organization. The solution is to diversify the risk by entering into foreign markets and enabling multiple streams of income. Diversify not only for weather or political events, but also to engage in multiple business cycles: China, Europe, South America, India, and the United States do not all have the same cycle or domestic demand growth. Again, what is the risk of not expanding?

The international markets offer exceptional expansion opportunities to stay true to your positioning, core values, and value curve. Instead of diluting the competitive advantages you've earned domestically to attract new customers, keep the core of your offerings and find where the customers are. The 'lowest common denominator' quest for clients is not the strategic plan for your company, expand overseas and find more of the customers you wish to target.

Step-by-Step Expansion Plan

International expansion does not need to be exceptionally complicated or difficult. Assembling the proper team of experts will be crucial to be in compliance with trade, labor, and tax laws. At a minimum, your organization will most likely need international tax attorneys, immigration attorneys, and local representation when appropriate for various contracts.

Market Research Options

The first step is obtaining market research on which markets to enter, and then more details once the particular regions are chosen. There are two basic forms of market research, the choice often depends on the budget, amount of time, and how much detail is necessary. The information to seek is wide ranging, but could include the largest growing markets, macro and micro trends for your category, best practices, current product use applications (eg: is this drill bit being used in a particular region or what companies are using drones and in what tasks or goals?), competitive players and standings, and traditional market demographics.

The most accurate and relevant, yet most expensive, is Primary research. It is original information often collected from a specialized company on contract for a particular scope. This includes interviews, field work, direct contacts, surveys, and should also include significant and up-to-date information.

Secondary research is a compilation of information obtained by other companies/organizations, and agencies (government and non-government) that is available either for fee or without cost, often found on the internet. There are many methods to gather this information, such as those listed on the below graphic "Secondary Research Methods." For example, the United States government generated and released statistics can be found on websites such as Export.gov[21] or USA.gov[22].

FIGURE 24: SECONDARY RESEARCH METHODOLOGIES

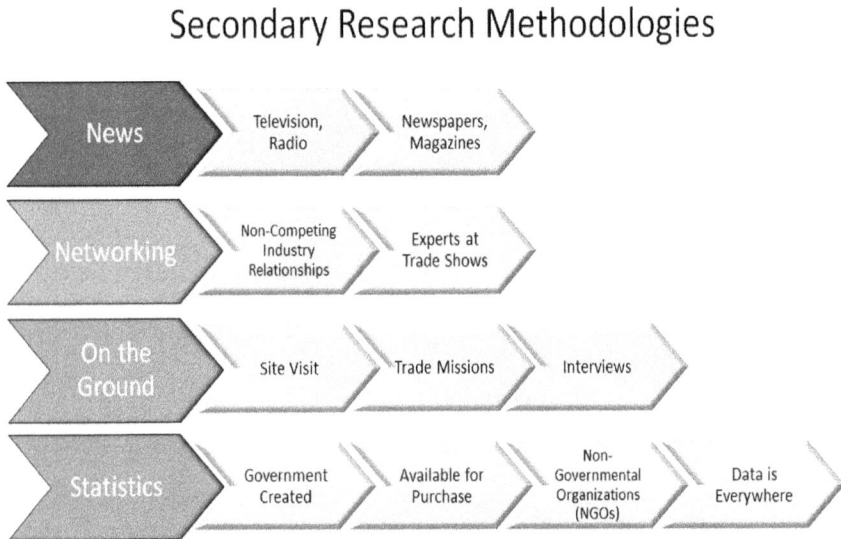

Secondary Research Methodologies

News	Television, Radio	Newspapers, Magazines		
Networking	Non-Competing Industry Relationships	Experts at Trade Shows		
On the Ground	Site Visit	Trade Missions	Interviews	
Statistics	Government Created	Available for Purchase	Non-Governmental Organizations (NGOs)	Data is Everywhere

A few notes of caution on Secondary research, the statistics are only as good as the numbers entered, and the methodology used to make calculations. There are different statistical standards in every country, and countries may not use the same methodologies to compute the same statistical categories. This can result in false-positive conclusions.

---

21   http://www.export.gov/
22   http://www.usa.gov/Business/Business-Data.shtml

Secondary data and research does not have as timely or completely up-to-date information as Primary data. If the statistics being used to make decisions are two years out of date, is that a considerable amount of time for the market in which you are focused? If in exceptionally financially turbulent areas such as Dubai or Brazil, how much time passes until economic or social statistics are no longer accurate and out of date?

The derivation of the statistics is also important when considering which type of firms are included. In many international economies, the Black Market is a powerful, yet undocumented force. Could your product be in competition with the Black Market and there are no accurate statistics to base decisions on? Additionally, are only large corporations counted in statistics, ignoring the legal and plentiful small to medium sized businesses?

Either method of research is appropriate, it is dependent upon the needed level of complexity, the amount of available resources, and the accuracy of the Secondary research. If you hire a market research company to perform Primary research, you will be aware of how the information is collected, what is, and is not, included, and can create a true market picture for accurate comparisons of country-to-country, or region-to-region for strategic decisions.

Strategic Positioning Approaches for the Foreign Market

There are multiple approaches or strategies to develop an overseas market for your product or service as summarized in the figure listed below. The first is to purchase an existing potential competitor and either rebrand to your own name and brand, or white-label the product using their existing brand that should have some market awareness.

FIGURE 25: METHODS TO DEVELOP NEW MARKETS

Methods to Develop New Markets

Joint Venture

Brokers & ETC/EMC

Purchase Existing Operations

International Expansion

Super Regional Office

Distribution Network

Open New Office

Hiring or contracting with a distribution network can create an efficient cost to productivity ratio by sharing risk, having a lower upfront cost, and sharing costs in fulfilling customer orders. However, the distribution network does not obtain new clients for your firm and will only service existing orders. The negatives in this relationship can be the distribution cost per transaction that may result in lower net profit, the lack of control on when and how the customers will be contacted (customer service), and that the efficiencies and execution are likely not to be as great as in the home country. There is also the risk of non-performance by the distribution network resulting in a waste of money, time, effort, and the potential of lost clientele.

With risk is reward, and there is no greater reward then having complete market penetration and maximizing profits by opening an office in the new market without the need of sharing profits or revenue with a partner or network. This will require the highest of upfront costs to transfer and hire staff, and to build awareness and sales in this new market. The firm will be tasked with all market research, distribution, and collections, tasks that can often be shared or administered by a partner or by another method. The ramp-up time can be long for all processes, networks, and sales cycles to come to fruition and to even create the initial revenue. Without a partner to help navigate the local laws and norms, there could be hurdles in culture and language, accounting & taxes, credit analysis, and the import/export process.

A super regional office is one foot in and one foot out. This is an office that generates sales in multiple countries or a geographic region without the cost and risk of physical locations or networks in each. For example, an organization may open an office in Panama City to create and service clients in neighboring and regional countries such as Colombia, Belize, Costa Rica, and Brazil. The organization is wider, but not necessarily deeper. If the clients can be obtained and serviced from the regional office in a cost efficient manner, and new business can be formed through effective marketing, then this can be a very productive methodology. Caveat emptor, there are many moving gears and barriers to success.

Brokers and agents, export trading companies (ETC), and export management companies (EMC) all serve as methods to obtain sales and new clients for the exporting company. The brokers and agents have a simpler mandate than the multifaceted ETCs and EMCs, and that is to sell product. Brokers typically have their own sales staff on the ground and are knowledgeable of the local market conditions, whereas an agent may be a single person operation. Often, the agent has a longer lasting relationship with the exporter and may represent several exporters concurrently as opposed to the broker, who often operates more short-term assignments and contracts. Brokers also charge commissions on sales and often retainers on services.

FIGURE 26: CREATING OVERSEAS CLIENTS

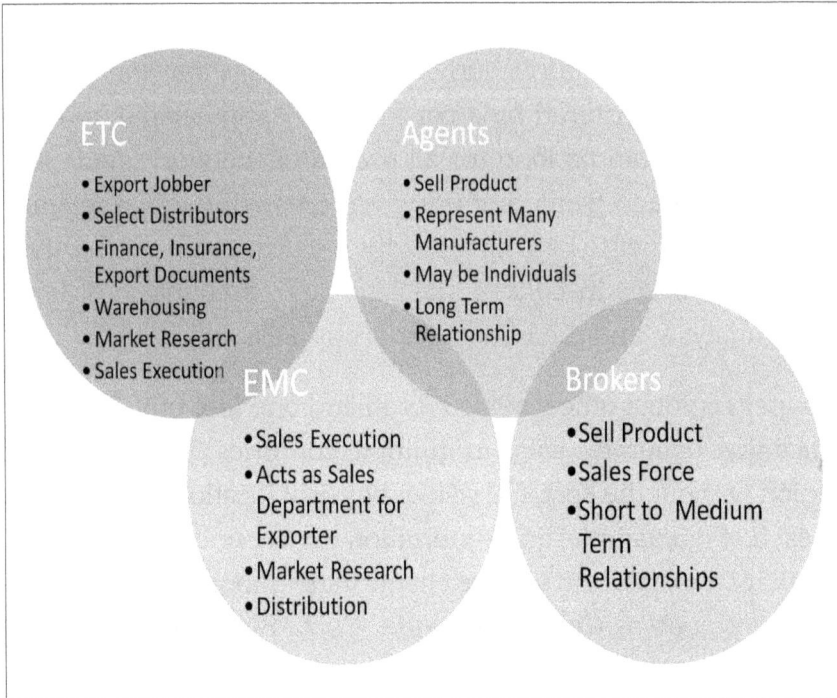

ETC
- Export Jobber
- Select Distributors
- Finance, Insurance, Export Documents
- Warehousing
- Market Research
- Sales Execution

Agents
- Sell Product
- Represent Many Manufacturers
- May be Individuals
- Long Term Relationship

EMC
- Sales Execution
- Acts as Sales Department for Exporter
- Market Research
- Distribution

Brokers
- Sell Product
- Sales Force
- Short to Medium Term Relationships

The export management companies(EMC) can act as a full service sales department for an exporter looking to enter a foreign market. They will handle all marketing, sales execution, and distribution within their already existing network for a faster entry. The upfront financial risk is relatively small except possible retainers, although the financial downsides are the commissions and potential discounting on future sales. There is risk in subcontracting control over the sales process and message/branding and positioning. With the increased fees due to commissions, the EMC, or ETC, could raise the product price outside of the proposed strategic landscape in which you have positioned the product to compete. As usual with any subcontracting, there is always a risk of non-performance.

The export trading companies (ETC) are often known as an 'export jobber' for they find purchasers who have needs first, and then find the appropriate exporter to supply this need. The ETC will then handle appropriate financing, insurance, export documents and any other service necessary for the sale and fulfillment of the order. The ETC also operates similarly to an EMC, fulfilling many of the basic duties to assist an export company find new clients for a fee.

For every layer of new hands in the till, it not only becomes more costly, but it is more likely complications will arise. Distribution networks add a new complexity where information could be lost, delayed, or altogether stopped. For example, if a customer in Kuala Lumpur requests a specific but complicated change to a small order of manufactured goods, this request will move from the client, to the distribution representative, to distribution management, to company headquarters, to the manufacturing facility and engineers, and then on the way back with hopefully fewer stops. Due to this game of telephone, it is no surprise if information is lost in distance and translation. Overcoming this type of shortfall begins with organization and decision making capability as discussed in Section Four.

Joint Ventures

The great advantage behind a Joint Venture (JV) operation is to share costs and risk in opening and developing new market(s), particularly partnering with those with local knowledge, expertise, and access. Not only could new connections from the partner open the door for faster or increased business, but the partner may also bring expertise in R&D, marketing, or another discipline to move the entire organization forward faster and further than without this new connection.

There are a few forms and methods to create a JV, beginning with the White Label model. The host country, or country headquarters wishes to export to, will (sometimes) manufacture and sell the product using a local name, and employ local workers. The exporting company will retain any trade secrets (like Coca Cola's secret formula) or patented technologies while the local partner develops the infrastructure, marketing plan, and all sales execution. This method can be very effective if the aim is to enter many markets within a short period with low upfront costs.

FIGURE 27: FORMS OF JOINT VENTURES

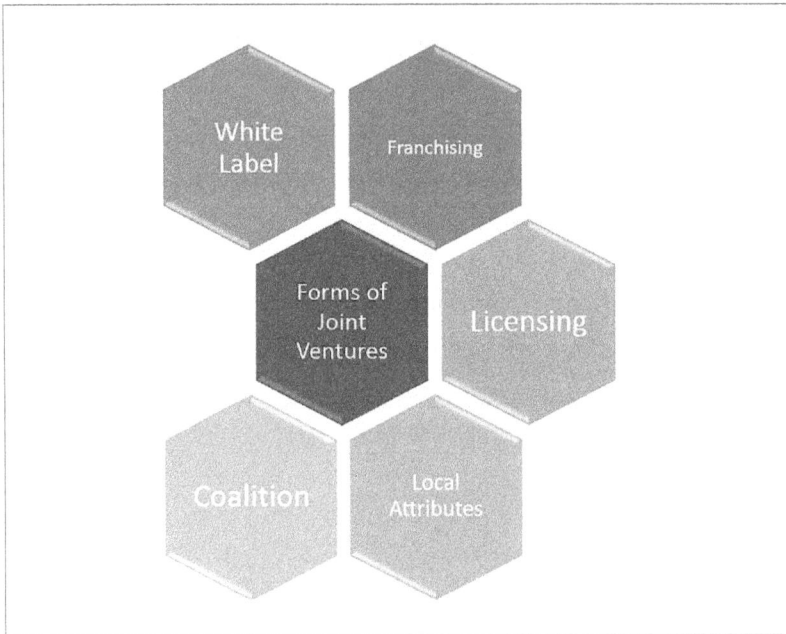

Franchising is effective when the goal is creating large scale brand awareness and to enter many markets within a short period of time. The risks are to find interested and qualified franchisees to purchase and operate the business, and then to develop the supporting infrastructure for successful operations. In many franchising operations, the franchisor often dictates the marketing strategy and the specifics towards execution. Additionally, the franchisor chooses the specific product offerings, including the timing and placement. This element should be considered twice when expanding internationally, ignoring or pushing aside local expertise may be a nail in the profitability coffin. For example, the world's flagship franchise model is McDonalds, with operations in over 100 countries; their menu differs from country to country to account for local tastes and customs. Hamburgers made from cow meat are not on offer in India, Vegemite makes an appearance in Australia, and the Shaka Shaka Chicken is sure to keep you coming back for more in Singapore.

By licensing the rights, brand/trademark, or intellectual property of an organization, there is limited direct financial risk to the home company, instead risk appears mostly in the form of ruined goodwill and theft of intellectual property (IP). If the controls and boundaries for the partner are not clearly set for how, where, and when they can use the licensed rights, it can result in the unintended consequence of brand diminishment through unforeseen actions. This usually can be avoided if the agreement is properly specified, albeit there are rarely protections sizeable enough if the host country operator does not act in good faith. The risk may be non-tangible in comparison to assets, property, or staff, but is still very formidable not only in immediate lost sales, but also opportunity cost for future sales due to theft of IP or diminished brand reputation. Coupled with the recognized risks, there is still a tremendous potential upside of high financial reward with little upfront export cost, especially for cutting edge technology.

'Local Attributes' are in combination with a local partner, creating a new business in the host country where each party shares in the ownership, manufacturing, sales & marketing strategy, execution, and costs. This is beneficial in establishing local best practices to best serve the market and to share the costs. This expertise can also assist in adjusting the product to meet local sensibilities. For example, automobile styles, size, and color differ greatly from America to Brazil, cigarettes are blended differently and packaged uniquely per country beyond just the language on the packaging and, more in depth, some kitchen equipment is designed to fit in the typical local kitchen size, not the average American kitchen with an abundance of space.

Control is still partially retained without delegating too much authority to partners, while still being able to learn and use their expertise. The financial risk exists, but yet is significantly less than if the home country would endeavor solo. Additionally, by partnering with the local expert, the home country may be able to enter multiple markets within a short period of time since much of the heavy lifting will be done in the host country, and mostly outbound cashflow is needed to finance the projects.

A Coalition is two or more companies coming together either for a project or more permanent operations. While working together, there may be a sharing of best practices, technology and, not least of all, risk. Since both companies will be contributing people, funds, and/or property (land, technology, etc.) to the project, this will create opportunities to work on larger projects than either company could handle on its own, or the risk to take on the project would be too great. Competitors are also aware of the power of a JV and often attempt to form their own to gain back some of the lost competitive advantage gained when two firms merge their resources.

Forming partnerships is common in the Oil & Gas industry; for example, ExxonMobil has formed a multi-billion dollar JV with Russian oil company Rosneft to develop offshore oil fields in the Black Sea and the Kara Sea. Rosneft sought technical expertise and execution, and ExxonMobil pursued revenue and profitable transactions.

Complications to Know & Avoid

Micro Factors to Control at Business Level

Not every company is successful when expanding to new markets overseas, but your company does not have to be one of the failures. Preparation and knowledge/awareness of the common stumbling blocks (so you are prepared to avoid them) are two of the keys for victory.

As discussed in Section Four, the decision making process must be clear and without ambiguity as to who has the authority to make the final decision, process steps, and how fast which decisions can or must be made. There should be complete clarity on the decision making roles and powers for the unit managers in the host country in comparison to the home country. When the decision making is in limbo, then the ability of the organization to expeditiously carry out its tasks and goals will be in jeopardy.

Navigating culture in the host country does not solely reside with the methods to obtain and retain new customers, it also includes approaches to communicate and be effective with staff, and the often overlooked relationship with local suppliers. Supplier relationships are vital for the organizations success and should be prioritized accordingly as mission critical assignments. In the home country, supplier relationships are often neglected due to heavy competition and the ability to replace one supplier with the next. In the host country, that luxury may not be available due to lack of either total number of suppliers, or of qualified suppliers. Develop the relationship to ensure smooth operations and to keep your organization a well-oiled machine.

Most countries differ in their own accepted norms and definition of 'customer service.' Do you believe that different standards for different countries is acceptable, welcome, and/or is a tautology? Training, incentivizing, and taking advantage of the Strategic Scorecard (see Section Four) to exhibit the Key Performance Indicators can turn your customer service staff into a winning team. Neglecting this important aspect of the company will often lead to misfortune.

First-rate market research should provide the exporting company with quality information and data in order to appropriately price their goods and services to the new market. Should the information be incomplete or of poor quality, and a wrong decision was subsequently made, all projections and corporate planning will be inaccurate and the entire strategy could be in jeopardy. Understanding the market pricing and the positioning of your products and services is key. Adjustments are of course welcome, but first there must be recognition of where the error and problems lie. This leads to execution of the strategy, a theme of this book. Execution is key whether it is performed in the home country, or in the host country. The fundamentals of having the vision, and working towards all believing, internalizing, and executing via their specific tasks, their unit goals, division goals, and company goals do not change.

Maintaining cost controls is an important factor in success. Although there should be complete planning before the international expansion, there are always unforeseen additional expenses that may occur, even before positive cashflow. Be aware that this is a reason why projects often do not get off the ground, or are delayed or are extremely over budget. During weekly or bi-weekly meetings, tackle the problems of increased costs and the potential to expand budgets before this becomes an insurmountable problem. Approach each problem with the foresight of recognizing that blown budgets may result in mission failure.

Macro Factors, Adapting at Country Level

The written and unwritten laws and policies of the host country can create insurmountable troubles for an exporter, although most can be worked with. If not, it is a simple strategic decision to not enter the country. We see this obvious decision often in countries like North Korea or some parts of Africa; although the newly intended market may not be as extreme as these examples there is still nothing wrong with walking away before throwing multiple eggs into that country's basket. Once again, the key to success is preparation and knowledge of the potential hurdles, whether they are Political Risk, Economic Risk, or Social Risk.

Political Risk

Political Risk measures the likelihood of loss resulting from a change in government policies, legislation, or military intervention or affairs. There are proactive steps to take to manage this political risk and not become a victim. The first and most important step is to be aware of the risk and chose countries judiciously. Argentina and Venezuela have significant recent histories of nationalization, currency difficulties (understatement), and corruption. Common sense would dictate the avoidance of countries with these current problems.

FIGURE 28: POLITICAL RISK & LEGAL HURDLES

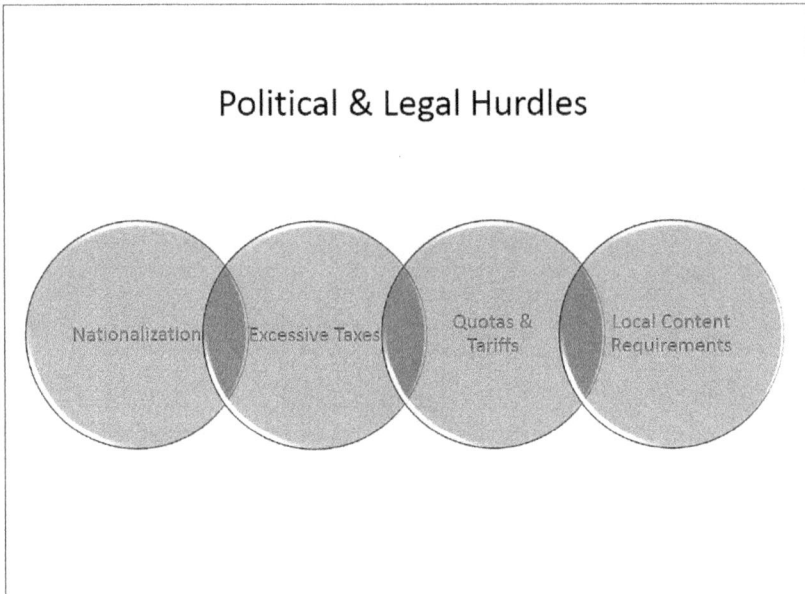

Political & Legal Hurdles

Nationalization | Excessive Taxes | Quotas & Tariffs | Local Content Requirements

Political Risk insurance policies may be purchased from major brokers to hedge against a possible loss; included are specific programs geared toward nationalization. Creating partnerships or Joint Ventures within the host country will insulate (to a degree) potential government or populist action against foreign or outside companies. The local partners can be the domestic face of the organization and not a faceless abstract of a "ruthless" multinational corporation.

Maintaining a low profile falls under the principle of 'out of sight, out of mind.' In the situation of governments who possess an adverse agenda for your quest, being unnoticed could be a blessing. This also encompasses being an excellent corporate citizen and not giving groups of environmentalists or labor unions reasons to take umbrage with your organization.

If you cannot beat them, join them. If your organization is very large and it is difficult to avoid the spotlight, then it is advised to form close relationships with the host country government. The government is less likely to make life difficult for their friends and those they trust and respect. This does not mean to join or create a Vichy government, but instead to respect their national sovereignty and work as a partner where appropriate.

If you are a partner or ally to those in government, and have a 'seat at the table' or are able to influence then you may be able to anticipate the blowing of the political winds and foresee changes that will affect your business plan and execution. With educated foresight, you can then make adjustments and continue to operate profitably.

Chevron has been able to operate in Argentina unobstructed and without suffering the similar fate of nationalization as industry colleague Repsol's subsidiary YPF in 2012. Since Chevron has annually increased oil production and YPF has suffered annual decreases, Chevron likely avoided the wrath of government due to this and their close relationship with the reigning administration.

The driving force in managing political risk is to become economically intertwined with the host country whereas any damage to your firm will be damage to the host country as well. To create this interdependency, create a large domestic supply chain and hire as many locals as possible. When the locals have an investment in your survival and well-being, then the government will listen and consider your point of view and needs before dictating potentially adverse policy.

Economic & Social Risk

What do Iran, Venezuela, and Argentina have in common? Official annual inflation is at least 10%, ranging up to 57% for Venezuela in 2014; this is not the club you wish to join. Also, consider the currency stability, and the macro movement of the standards of living, are they decreasing or rising rapidly, as in the case of Canada[23] and Syria (declining) or China (increasing)? It is important to understand the demographic information about a country for this will also likely be a preview of future policy and economic conditions.

In Nigeria, the country demographics are significantly skewed towards youth with well over 65% of the population under 25. How will tax revenue be generated? What will be the major drivers of government spending today, in five years, and in fifteen years? Which type of products will the population need today and in X amount of years looking forward? Think ahead to how your organization should position itself by studying the demographics.

FIGURE 29: NIGERIA POPULATION PYRAMID

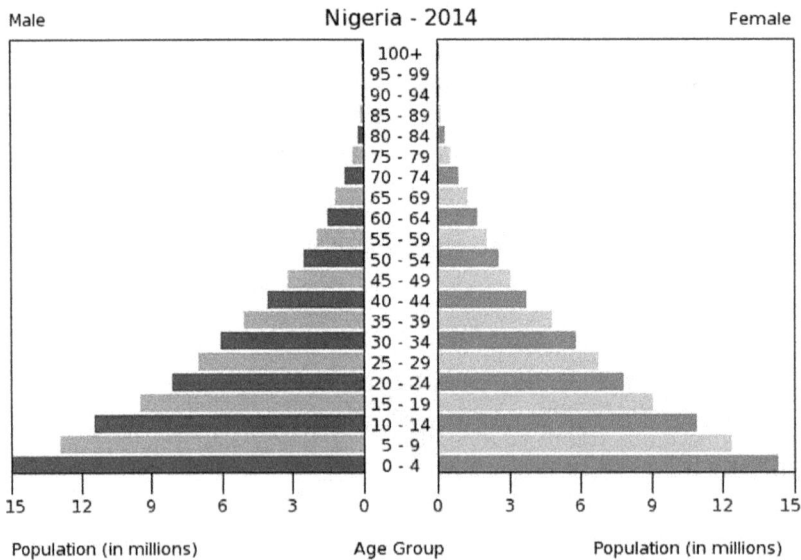

Consider the social risks of when large segments of the population are in their youth. Will this lead to large scale unemployment

---

23   From 1976 to 2013, there was an inflation adjusted cost of housing increase of 76% and the real household income rose only 5%. Additionally the female percentage active in the workforce rose from 54% of the population to 82% and male rates stayed level. More hours, less house, lowered standard of living (Kershaw n.d.).
24   Source: CIA Factbook, https://www.cia.gov/library/publications/the-world-factbook/fields/2010.html

and millions of youth on the street desperately seeking income, food, shelter, and a sense of being? This social and demographical risk could turn into a political storm (see the Middle East for endless examples).

In comparison, Japan has a significantly older population. Same questions as with Nigeria, how will tax revenues be generated and where will the government spending focus? What products and services will the market be demanding today and in the future? What are the social risks inherent with an older population and how may this effect the business strategy and execution?

FIGURE 30: JAPAN POPULATION PYRAMID

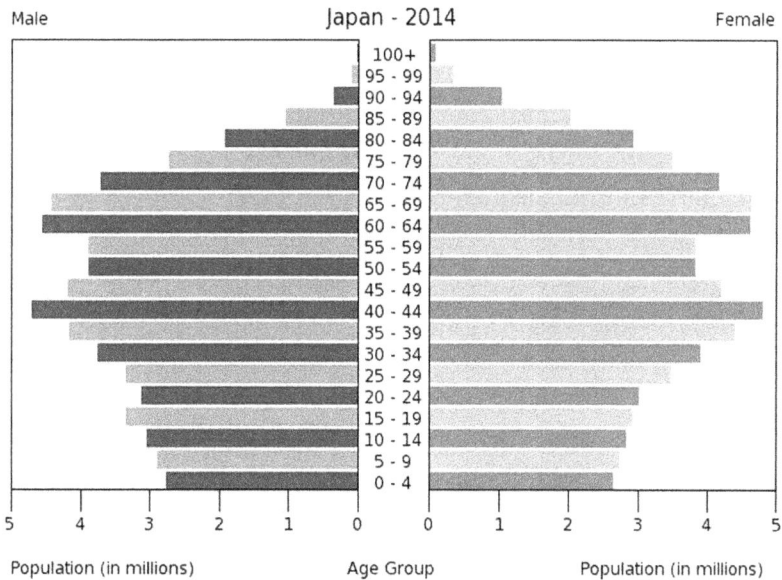

Common Issues

This international section of the book has emphasized the need to

25   Source: CIA Factbook, https://www.cia.gov/library/publications/the-world-factbook/fields/2010.html

acquire and maintain local knowledge and influential contacts to reduce risk and to ensure smooth strategy execution. Additionally, this local expertise can assist with the social and cultural factors in the sales and marketing process. Remember the Shaka Shaka Chicken in Singapore based McDonalds? Local sensitivities and knowledge helped generate this product and avoid potential pitfalls in the way products are received and perceived by the general population. This can also include language in advertising, face-to-face customer service or sales, or executive level relations between companies. Every culture has its own etiquettes, nuances, and norms in negotiations and in general business practices.

Always adapt to the local custom, and do not force your own values or culture upon potential clients or employees, it is often a rude awakening when this fails.

British multinational bank HSBC ran a multiyear advertising campaign positioning itself as purveyors of the world's customs, culture, and local knowledge due to their numerous international branches. The tag line is (or was) 'The Worlds Local Bank' to help international businesses navigate the complexities of culture, perception and, of course, banking.

FIGURE 31: HSBC, PEOPLE VALUE THINGS DIFFERENTLY

Not every host country or nation has the same developed infrastructure as the home country. This could include utilities (electric, water, internet, telephone) or supply chain (roads, trains, ports) that will result in frequent delays, and being on-time may only exist in a memory or a dream. Before beginning on the endeavor, factor the likely infrastructure shortcomings into the strategy and plan and do not be surprised when inevitable disappointment arrives. Do not make assumptions about the infrastructure based upon your own standards and expectations, be honest in the assessment of the existing networks.

Global Decision Making

In international expansion there are often time zones, oceans, and cultures to complicate strategy execution. Having a plan to create a fast decision making process between the expansion and the headquarters will be critical. With a Joint Venture in any of its various forms (including franchising, coalitions, etc.) there may be complications as to who really has the authority and ability to make decisions and to execute them. This should be made explicitly clear before commencing the project and the process should follow as designed.

When working with a host country partner, who creates the guidelines for business processes, employment manuals, and/or workplace or factory conditions? Next, who decides how the guidelines are to be implemented and would have final say over the renting or purchasing of a property? Must both parties come to an agreement on both cost and location, or is only cost a factor by the headquarters?

Do home country labor rules and laws apply to the host country? Technically no, a worker in India does not have the same legal protections as an American worker in Florida regardless if they are employed by the same company or via subsidiaries of the same parent organization. How about morally?

Are clothing retailers Benetton and Walmart who source products

globally responsible for the building conditions, wages, and overall employee well-being in every country? In April 2013 the Rana
Plaza factory/building in Dhaka, Bangladesh collapsed killing
1,130 of the workers inside. In the situation of Rana Plaza, cracks
in the foundation appeared the day before the collapse leading to
the bank on the ground floor and a few other organizations vacat-
ing the building. Who made the decision to send garment workers into the building the next day? Was that local, or at the home
country (if there was one)? Who is responsible, and who should
make these decisions for the home countries best interest?

Before declaring that all decisions should be made at the headquarters where things can be "trusted," and perhaps be economically more efficient to necessitate a smaller overall number of
managers, there are compelling reasons to allow for local decision making as well. Remember, if your staff cannot make quality
decisions, they should not be members of your staff. Good managers make good decisions, bad managers make bad decisions.

Determine in advance which decisions can be delegated and
which headquarters must have control over. For example, if a
product is being manufactured in the host country but is to be
sold and consumed in the home country, how much flexibility
should be granted in changing the product specifications, aes-
thetic, design, materials, or packaging in the name of efficiency?
Is it possible that a host country manager could find a lighter plastic for a significant savings over the current heavy plastic used
in the product design? If so, is he a hero for the bottom line savings, or a villain for 'destroying' the product? This can be avoided
with a clear set of parameters on what can be decided locally, and
which choices need approval from headquarters.

Before developing the parameters, take into consideration that
managers in the field who are close to the business process,
whether that is in sales, manufacturing, or procurement, should
have a large amount of data and information to make informed

decisions about their local market and operations. Although executives at headquarters can see the big picture across multiple units and regions, the local unit manager can see what affects their market most clearly. Allowing this local manager to make some decisions increases the nimbleness of the firm, and allows those with the most local knowledge to be responsible for the direction moving forward.

A major car manufacturer created a worldwide purchasing group to streamline and create economies-of-scale but, at the same time, tried to integrate the local purchasers per region for input and logistical purposes. Some parts were built exclusively in Mexico and shipped to both the European and the Asian assembly lines, whereas the finer materials and textiles for the interior were sourced locally in-country. This blending of global vs local was effective and successful for it created economies-to-scale, and because there was a clear decision making process and determination on who has the responsibility to source items that reside in an ambiguous jurisdiction between the purchasing groups. For these items it was clear who has the final decision and the criteria was clear and transparent on how the decision was to be reached. Since the decision making criteria was open for all to see, less conflict arose between the two sometimes competing departments.

Section Summary & Conclusion

International expansion is a significant opportunity to greatly increase revenue and long-term stability for a firm. With the increased risk, there is a considerable reward. However, the risk factors can be managed with proper planning, research, and developing the right people in the proper place. There is a myriad of potential methods for international expansion, and certainly a proper fit for each firm based on its risk profile and medium to long-term goals.

A firm is only as successful as the staff, the strategy, and the execution whether in a domestic market or international expansion.

Below are the fundamental concepts and actionable items presented in this Section:

1. The vast majority of the world's population resides outside the United States; focusing on only one market severely limits revenue potential.

2. International expansion is an opportunity to create partnerships to share risk, costs, and even gain in R&D expertise and equipment.

3. International expansion is a form of reducing risk by diversification. This is no longer dependent on a singular business cycle or domestic macroeconomic, and/or event driven factors.

4. Before expanding into new markets, obtain as much intelligence through market research (Primary and/or Secondary research) as possible.

    a. Be mindful of the caveats of the Secondary research

5. There are several methods to develop new markets:

    a. Joint Venture (various subsets), purchase of existing operations, establishing a distribution network, opening overseas offices both in country and supra-regionally, hiring EMCs (export management companies) and ETCs (export trading companies)

    b. Joint Ventures have a range of forms and structures that allows firms to share risks, expertise, and pool together for comparative and competitive advantages.

6. Navigating local culture is a critical success factor in employee/employer relations, supplier relations, and the various touch points of customer service, client interaction, and marketing.

7. Cost control abilities and business transaction norms may be significantly different than in the home country.

8. Political, Economic, and Social Risk are all hurdles that need to be evaluated before entering a market, and through proper planning can be effectively managed.

9. Relationships with local government (where appropriate) can be helpful in foreseeing significant changes to the business environment due to shifting political winds.

10. Demographics are the start of the conversation and evaluation. They provide a clear window into the current challenges and opportunities, in addition to the future wants and needs of a nation.

11. Develop a global decision making model to (1) increase accountability and efficiencies, and (2) to be unambiguous between partners (or companies, ventures, etc.) as to who is responsible and possesses the authority to make decisions on a range of issues, including: labor conditions and relations, product details, pricing, marketing.

Conclusion

This has been a concise journey through the most relevant information for organizations to determine the meaning behind their work, to decide where they want to go, and how to reach that all-encompassing vision. THE PROFIT HAS been a step-by-step guide, following the advice will aid you in achieving success. If your organization requires more assistance, contact the author.

Just to show the author has a sense of humor about the consulting business, here are a few nuggets for enjoyment:

There was a glass of water on the table...
One man says, "It's half full." He is an optimist.
Second man says, "It's half empty." He is a pessimist.
Third man says, "It's twice too big." He is a
management consultant.

An efficiency expert concluded his lecture with a note of caution.
"Don't try these techniques at home."
"Why not?" asked somebody from the audience.
"I watched my wife's routine at breakfast for years," the expert
explained. "She made lots of trips between the fridge, stove, table
and cabinets, often carrying a single item at a time. One day I

told her, "You're wasting too much time. Why don't you try carrying several things at once?"

"Did it save time?" the guy in the audience asked.

"Actually, yes," replied the expert. "It used to take her 20 minutes to make breakfast. Now I do it in ten."

The classified ad said, "Wanted: CEO needs a one armed consultant, with an MBA and five years of experience."

The man who won the job asked, "I understand most of the qualifications you required, but why 'one armed'?"

The CEO answered, "I have had many consultants, and I am tired of hearing with each advice the phrase 'on the other hand'."

Tell the maître 'd,

good supply chain management

will speed the slow service.

Table of Figures

Figure 1: Hewlett-Packard 35, from 1972 ... 36

Figure 2: Annual Strategy Attempts Fail ... 44

Figure 3: Business Model Concepts ... 54

Figure 4: Simple Value Curve ... 67

Figure 5: Simple Value Curve ... 68

Figure 6: Value Curve, Technology Package ... 76

Figure 7: Is the Differentiation in the Market Sustainable? ... 79

Figure 8: Framework to Perfect Value Curve ... 80

Figure 9: Value Curve Three ... 81

Figure 10: Three Tiers of Customers, Find the commonalities between the three groups ... 85

Figure 11: Strategy Education Methodology ... 91

Figure 12: Strategic Scorecard ... 93

Figure 13: Effective Decision Making ... 108

Figure 14: Framework to Evaluate Previous Decision Making ... 110

Figure 15: Barriers to Market Adoption ... 114

Figure 16 Google's core offering opens the video, typing in a keyword search before the emotional jorney begins ... 118

Figure 17: Framework to Find the Emotion ... 120

Figure 18 Touching, emotive, but where is the Drink? ... 123

Figure 19: Woodford Reserve 'Run for the Roses' Mint Julep Cup ... 128

Figure 20: Keys for an Effective Trigger 130

Figure 21: The product should be seen, so it can be imitated 132

Figure 22: Sales Improvement Strategy Process 139

Figure 23: Methods to Motivate Staff 145

Figure 24: Secondary Research Methodologies 158

Figure 25: Methods to Develop New Markets 160

Figure 26: Creating Overseas Clients 162

Figure 27: Forms of Joint Ventures 164

Figure 28: Political Risk & Legal Hurdles 170

Figure 29: Nigeria Population Pyramid 172

Figure 30: Japan Population Pyramid 174

Figure 31: HSBC, People Value Things Differently 174

Bibliography

2014. *American Public Transportation Association.* June . http://www.apta.com/Pages/default.aspx.

Aulet, Bill. 2013. *Disciplined Entrepreneurship: 24 Steps to a Successful Startup.* Wiley.

Awe, Susan. 2009. *Going Global: An Information Sourcebook for Small and Medium-Sized Businesses.* 1st. Libraries Unlimited.

Berger, Jonah. 2013. *Contagious: Why Things Catch On.* Simon & Schuster.

Blank, Steve. 2013. *The Four Steps to the Epiphany.* 2nd. K&S Ranch.

Breeze, Hannah. 2014. *Microsoft: Customers trust us much less since NSA scandal.* London: Incisive Financial Publishing Limited. http://www.channelweb.co.uk/crn-uk/news/2351267/microsoft-customers-trust-us-much-less-since-nsa-scandal.

Bucheli, Marcelo, and Ruth V Aguilera. 2010. "Political Survival, Energy Policies, and Multinational Corporations." *Management International Review*, May 18: 347-378.

Bughin, Jacques, Jonathan Doogan, and Ole Jorgen Vetvik. 2010. "A new way to measure word-of-mouth marketing." *McKinsey Quarterly.* http://www.mckinsey.com/insights/marketing_sales/a_new_way_to_measure_word-of-mouth_marketing.

2014. *Business Data & Statistics.* July. http://www.usa.gov/Business/Business-Data.shtml.

Carrillo, Patricia. 2004. "Managing Knowledge: Lessons from the oil and gas sector." *Construction Management & Economics*, July: 631-642.

Charles, Deborah, and Warren Strobel. 2013. *With troops and techies, U.S. prepares for cyber warfare.* Washington, DC: Reuters. http://www.reuters.com/article/2013/06/07/us-usa-cyberwar-idUS-BRE95608D20130607.

Christensen, Clayton M. 2011. *The Innovator's Dilemma: The Revolutionary Book That Will Change the Way You Do Business.* HarperBusiness.

Croll, Alistair, and Benjamin Yoskovitz. 2013. *Lean Analytics: Use Data to Build a Better Startup Faster.* O'Reilly Media.

David, Pierre A., and Richard D. Stewart. 2010. *International Logistics: Management of International Trade Operations.* 3rd . Atomic Dog.

Davies, Matt. 2010. "Inorganic Growth." *Business Strategies*, June / July: 14-16.

2014. *Deepwater Horizon oil spill.* http://en.wikipedia.org/wiki/Deepwater_Horizon_oil_spill.

2014. *Distribution of the population according to age, by Country.* July. https://www.cia.gov/library/publications/the-world-factbook/fields/2010.html.

Ewart, Stephen. 2014. "Red Ocean blues challenge Poseidon." *Calgary Herald*, March 25.

2014. *Federal Tax Law Keeps Piling Up.* June . http://www.cch.com/TaxLaw-PileUp.pdf.

Fletcher, Richard, and Heather Crawford. 2014. *International Marketing: An Asia-Pacific Perspective.* Pearson Australia.

2014. *FracMapper.* June. Accessed June 2014. http://www.fractracker.org/map/.

Gadiesh, Orit, and James L Gilbert. 2001. "Frontline Action." *Harvard Business Review*, May: 72-79.

Giammona, Craig. 2013. "Hess successfully shrinks itself to grow." *Fortune Magazine*, December 4. http://fortune.com/2013/12/04/hess-successfully-shrinks-itself-to-grow/.

Girotra, Karen, and Seguei Netessine. 2014. "Four Paths to Business Model Innovation." *Harvard Business Review* 98-103.

Gladwell, Malcolm. 2000, 2002. *The Tipping Point, How Little Things Can Make a Big Difference.* New York: Little, Brown & Company.

2013. *Google Zeitgeist | Here's to 2013.* Youtube.com. Google.com. doi:http://bit.ly/1elrE4A.

Graham, John L, and Philip R. Cateora. 1998. *International Marketing.* Richard D Irwin.

Graham, Paul. 2014. *Paul Graham Quotations.* June. http://www.
    brainyquote.com/quotes/authors/p/paul_graham.html.

Grant, Robert M. 2003. "Strategic Planning in a Turbulent Environment:
    Evidence from the Oil Majors." *Strategic Management Journal*, 491-
    517.

Gray, Dave, Sunni Brown, and James Macanufo. n.d. *Gamestorming: A
    Playbook for Innovators, Rulebreakers, and Changemakers.* O'Reilly
    Media.

Guillebeau, Chris. 2012. *The $100 Startup: Reinvent the Way You Make a
    Living, Do What You Love, and Create a New Future.* First. Crown
    Business.

Hill, Charles W. L. , Peter Hwang, and W Chan Kim. 1990. "An Eclectic Theory
    of the Choice of International Entry Mode." *Strategic Management
    Journal*, May 19: 117-128.

2014. *Homepage.* July. http://www.export.gov/.

Inkpen, Andrew, and Michael H Moffett. 2011. *The Global Oil & Gas Industry:
    Management, Strategy and Finance.* PennWell Corp.

Johnson, Mark, Clayton Christensen, and Henning Kagerman. 2008. "Rein-
    venting Your Business Model." *Harvard Business Review* 50-59.

Kaplan, Saul. 2012. *The Business Model Innovation Factory: How to Stay Rel-
    evant When The World is Changing.* Wiley.

Kawasaki, Guy. 2012. *Enchantment: The Art of Changing Hearts, Minds, and
    Actions.* Portfolio Trade.

—. 2000. *Rules for Revolutionaries: The Capitalist Manifesto for Creating and
    Marketing New Products and Services.* HarperBusiness.

—. 2004. *The Art of the Start: The Time-Tested Battle-Hardened Guide for
    Anyone Starting Anything.* Portfolio Hardcover.

Kawasaki, Guy, and Shawn Welch. 2013. *APE: Author, Publisher, Entrepreneur.*
    1st. Nononina Press.

Kershaw, Paul. n.d. *Declining Standard of Living.* Vers. http://gensqueeze.
    ca/. http://blogs.ubc.ca/newdealforfamilies/declining-standard-of-
    living/.

Kim, W. Chan, and Renee Mauborgne. 2009. "How Strategy Shapes Struc-
    ture." *Harvard Business Review*, September: 72-80.

—. 2004. "Value Innovation: The Strategic Logic of High Growth." *Harvard Business Review*, July.

Kim, W. Chan, and Renee Mauborgne. 2014. "Blue Ocean Leadership." *Harvard Business Review*, May: 60-72.

Lafley, A.G. 2013. *Playing to Win: How Strategy Really Works.* First. Harvard Business Review Press.

Landrum, Nancy E. 2008. "Murphy Oil and the El Dorado Promise: A Case of Strategic Philanthropy." *Journal of Business Inquiry*, 79-85.

Masterson, Adam K. 2014. *Business Model Generation: The Blueprints Every Entrepreneur in Every Industry Needs Today to Achieve Maximum Profits.* Amazon Digital Services, Inc.

Mauborgne, Renee, and W. Chan Kim. 2003. "Tipping Point Leadership." *Harvard Business Review*, April: 60-69.

McCracken, Harry. 2014. "How Gmail Happened: The Inside Story of its Launch 10 Years Ago." *Time Magazine.* http://time.com/43263/gmail-10th-anniversary/.

Neilson, Gary L, Karla L Martin, and Elizabeth Powers. 2008. "The Secrets to Successful Strategy Execution." *Harvard Business Review*, June: 60-70.

Nokia. 2014. *Nokia.* http://company.nokia.com/en.

Norton, David P, and Robert S Kaplan. 1996. "Using the Balanced Scorecard as a Strategic Management System." *Harvard Business Review*, January - February: 150-161.

Nudd, Tim. 2013. *The 10 Best Ads of 2013.* Vers. bit.ly/WhtPPv. December. Accessed July 2014. http://www.adweek.com/news-gallery/advertising-branding/10-best-ads-2013-154404#intro.

Osterwalder, Alexander, and Yves Pigneur. 2010. *Business Model Generation: A Handbook for Visionaries, Game Changers, and Challengers.* John Wiley & Sons.

Pancero, Jim. 2005. *You Can Always Sell More: How to Improve Any Sales Force.* Wiley.

Patton, Mike. 2014. "The Three Countries With The Highest Inflation." *Forbes.* http://www.forbes.com/sites/mikepatton/2014/05/09/the-three-countries-with-the-highest-inflation/.

Porras, Jerry I, and James C Collins. 1996. "Building Your Company's Vision."

Harvard Business Review, September - October: 65-77.

Porter, Michael. 2008. "The Five Competitive Forces That Shape Strategy." *Harvard Business Review* 78-93.

Porter, Michael. 1996. "What is Strategy." *Harvard Business Review* 61-78.

Reckhenrich, Jorg, Jamie Anderson, and Martin Kupp. 2009. "The Shark is Dead, How to Build a New Market." *Business Strategy Review*, Winter: 40-47.

Renee, Mauborgne, and W. Chan Kim. 2005. *Blue Ocean Strategy.* Boston, Massachusetts: Harvard Business School Publishing Corporation.

Cut, Joe Guest @ Final, The Mill, and Barry Ackroyd, . 2013. *Robinsons 'Pals'.* Vers. https://www.youtube.com/watch?v=gVY220ECU2A. Dom Thomas and Lizie Gower. May 3. Accessed July 2014. bit.ly/1l3qIzN.

Rogers, Paul, and Marcia Blenko. 2006. "Who Has the D?" *Harvard Business Review* 52-61.

Sandhusen, Richard L. 1997. *International Marketing.* Barron's Educational Seres.

Steele, Michael Mankins & Richard. 2009. "Turning Great Strategy into Great Performance." *Harvard Business Review* 64-72.

2014. *The Water Project, About Us.* http://thewaterproject.org/about_us.

2013. *Tuition costs of colleges and universities.* http://nces.ed.gov/fastfacts/display.asp?id=76.

Vivoda, Vlado. 2011. "Bargaining Model for the International Oil Industry." *Business and Politics* (Berkeley Electronic Press).

Wall, Robert. 2013. "Emirates Orders Additional 50 Airbus A380s to Expand Fleet." *Bloomberg.*

2014. *Woodfor Reserve.* May. Accessed June 14th, 2014. https://www.woodfordreservemintjulep.com/the-cups/.

Zenger, John H, Joseph R Folkman, and Scott K Edinger. 2011. "Making Yourself Indispensable." *Harvard Business Review*, October: 84-92.

Index

80/20 rule, 138, 148

A.G. Lafley, 102

A380 superjumbo jets, 59

Accountability, 91

Adweek, 120

Affordable Care Act, 113

Africa, 13, 166

Airbus, 59, 187

Alessandra Ambrosio, 30

Amazon, 23, 186

American Express, 122

Apathy, 113

Apple, 26, 30

Appraisal, 113

Arduous, 113

asteroid, 20, 21

AT&T, 31, 36

Avenue, 12, 114

Avis, 122

Awareness, 112, 126

Bangkok, Thailand, 94

Bargaining Power of Buyers, 29

Bargaining Power of Suppliers, 29

Barnes & Nobles, 23

Benetton, 173

Best Buy, 30, 32, 46, 121

Bloomberg, 31

Bluetooth, 73, 78

BMW, 117

Boeing, 35

Bourbon, 125

BP, 55, 95, 97

cheesecake, 34

Chevy, 123

Circuit City, 32

City School Teachers, 32

Cloud Services, 121

cloud storage, 35

Constitution, 13

core ideology, 13, 14, 18

Core Ideology, 13, 14, 18, 23, 89

corporate communications, 113

Cost Structure, 54

CRM, 144

customer value proposition, 52

Decision Making Bottleneck, 102

Deepwater Horizon, 95, 97

Delta Airlines, 35

Deployment Game, 98

Descriptives, 121, 122

Devil's Advocate, 99

DirecTV, 36

Dish, 36

Don Draper, 12, 15

Douglas B. Reeves, 87

Dubai, 58, 156

Emirates Airline, 58

Expedia, 35

Exploration and Production, 26

ExxonMobil, 26, 55, 131, 164

FABs, 111

Facebook, 25

Features, Advantages, & Benefits,
116

FedEx, 35

Four Seasons, 115

Fracking, 58

Friends, 87

FTP, 35

GE, 16

Geek Squad, 121

General Motors, 76, 100

Gisele Bundchen, 30

Goal Setting, 18

Google, 21, 55, 115

Gulf of Mexico, 25, 95

Guy Kawasaki, 46, 75, 99

Halliburton, 95

Hallmark, 120

handheld calculator, 33

Harry Truman, 44

Henry Ford, 20

Home Depot, 59

Hong Kong, 94

Huntsman, 65, 66, 73, 78, 79

Hydraulic Fracturing, 58

Ikea, 27

Inspirational Jump, 97

intellectual property, 32

iPhone, 30

jigsaw puzzles, 113

joint value creation, 102

Joint Value Creation, 28

Kayak, 38

Kentucky Derby, 104, 125

key processes, 52

Key Processes, 55

key resources, 41, 52

Key Resources, 54

Kim & Mauborgne, 74, 77

Legos, 113

Leverage, 31, 33, 145, 146, 147

Limited Brands, 30

Lowes, 59

Mad Men, 12, 15

Malaysia, 102

Mark Johnson, 52

market adoption, 113, 114

Market Adoption, 112

market barriers, 112

Marketing, 111

McDonald's, 43

McDonalds, 83, 85

Michael Hayden, 12

Michael Porter, 27

Microsoft, 26

minivan, 75, 80

Mint Julep Cup, 125

Mission Statement, 22, 23, 24, 25, 48, 89

nanotechnology, 32

National Basketball Association

NBA, 145

National Security Agency, 12, 120

NetJets, 20

New York Public Library, 23

Nobel Prize, 44

Nokia, 11

NSA, 12, 120

ObamaCare, 113

Old Friends Retirement Center, 125

Orbitz, 35

Pareto Principle, 148

Paul Buchheit, 55

Paul Graham, 51

Peter Drucker, 52

pharmaceutical, 32

Phil Kolter, 111

pipeline, 32

poker, 146

Porter, Michael, 187

PowerPoint, 42, 117

Procter & Gamble, 28, 101

profit formula, 52

Profit Formula, 53, 54, 56, 57, 60

proppants, 58

Railroad Engineers, 32

Reluctant group, 81

Resource Velocity, 54

Reuters, 12

Revenue Model, 54

Risk & Reward Hurdle, 97

Robinsons, 120

Rockstar Energy Drink, 123

Roger, 9, 14, 17, 23, 24, 25, 36, 55, 56

Roger Harrison, 9, 14

Roy H. Williams, 111

Run for the Roses, 125

Sanjeev Singh, 55

Satellite TV, 36

scorecard, 42

Segmentation, 80

Seinfeld, 87

Seoul, South Korea, 94

shipping company, 14

Simon Mainwaring, 11

Skype, 35

social media, 45

Sony, 32, 46

Southwest Airlines, 16

Southwestern Energy, 14

Sports Utility Vehicle

SUV, 80

Sprint, 31

Status Quo Mindset, 97

Strategic Principle, 15, 16, 17, 18, 23

strategic principles, 46

Strategic Scorecard, 90, 94, 100, 142, 165

Strategic Vision, 89

Strategy Performance, 37

SUV, 80

Symbian Operating System, 11

Taco Bell, 123

Target, 28

The Five A's, 112

The Water Project, 13

Thomson Reuters, 31

Threat of New Entrants, 29

Threat of Substitute Products or Services, 29

Transocean, 95

Travel agents, 35

Tropicana, 123

Unfamiliar group, 83

United States, 2, 12, 13, 32, 35, 36, 44, 58, 59, 122, 153, 154

United States Marine Corps, 122

United States Postal Service, 35

United States Tax Code, 44

UPS, 35

value curve, 63, 64, 65, 66, 68, 70, 72, 73, 74, 75, 78, 79, 84

Verizon, 31

Victoria's Secret, 30, 127

Virginia, 94

VOIP, 82

Volkswagen, 122

Walkman, 32

Wal-Mart, 15, 18, 28

weight room guy, 92, 93

Werther's, 123

Western Governors University, 57, 81

WGU, 57, 81

whiskey, 12

Woodford Reserve, 125

YouTube, 116, 120

Zeitgeist, 115

www.ingramcontent.com/pod-product-compliance
Lightning Source LLC
Chambersburg PA
CBHW060550210326
41519CB00014B/3430